WOMEN
at the Well

Expressions of faith, life and worship
drawn from our own wisdom

Prepared for the Womaen's Caucus
of the Church of the Brethren

Compiled by

Betty Jo Buckingham

and

Jean Lichty Hendricks

Edited by

Betty Jo Buckingham

Womaen's Caucus of the Church of the Brethren
Elgin, Illinois • 1987

Women at the Well

Expressions of faith, life and worship drawn from our own wisdom

Printed in the United States of America.

Library of Congress Cataloging-in-Publication Data

Women at the Well.

1. Women—Prayer-books and devotions—English.
I. Buckingham, Betty Jo. II. Hendricks, Jean Lichty.
BV4844.W65   1987   242'.643   87-6224

ISBN 0-9618243-0-1 (pbk)

Quotations from or references to the following titles are used by
permission of copyright holders:

Julia Esquival, *Threatened with Resurrection*, Brethren Press,
1982.

Savina J. Teubal, *Sarah the Priestess: The First Matriarch of
Genesis*, Swallow Press, (Athens, Ohio) 1984.

Thorkild Jacobsen, *The Treasures of Darkness: A History of
Mesopotamian Religion*, Yale University Press, 1976.

Midrash Rabbah, Soncino Press, 1951.

Helen S. Peterson, *Sojourner Truth, Fearless Crusader*, Garrard, 1972.

Dale Spender, *Women of Ideas: And What Men Have Done to
Them*, Methuen, Inc., 1984.

Lillian Smith, *Killers of the Dream*, W. W. Norton and Company,
Inc., © 1949; © 1961 by Lillian Smith.

Rachel C. Wahlberg, *Jesus According to a Woman*, Paulist
Press, 1975.

Peggy Gibble-Keenan, "I Am Somebody."

Ingrid Rogers, "The Stone Wall," (a play); "The Wall," (words
and music).

Printed by
Good Printers, Inc.
Bridgewater, VA

Dedication

The Womaen's Caucus of the Church of the Brethren is dedicated to improving the position of women in the Church of the Brethren in the universal church and in the world. For that reason the Caucus rejoices whenever the leadership of strong women is offered and received. Many such women have contributed to women's organizations within the church and to the Womaen's Caucus of the Church of the Brethren. We acknowledge our debt to this "cloud of witnesses."

One woman has especially opened a new page to women in the Church of the Brethren by being the first woman to be appointed to an executive position in the Church of the Brethren General Offices. Ruby Rhoades served with style and wisdom as executive for the World Ministries program of the Church before cancer forced her retirement and brought on her death. We rejoice that her illness and other responsibilities did not prevent her from contributing one of the units of this book. It would be less than complete without her contribution.

Because Ruby Rhoades serves as such a good example and representative of this "cloud of witnesses" and because of her own invaluable witness, we feel privileged to dedicate WOMEN AT THE WELL to Ruby Rhoades.

Women At The Well

Preface

The Church of the Brethren Womaen's Caucus has felt the need to provide utterance for the tongueless ones, for those limited and left searching by traditional devotional materials with masculine terms for God and humankind. That offering, that utterance is this book, WOMEN AT THE WELL.

We planned this book to provide a personal devotional resource based on scripture which returns to women words to help express their self-identity and their images of God. We offer this book to our sisters in the Church of the Brethren and in the wider world. While it was conceived as a personal worship resource, many of the devotions were prepared for group worship and most of the more personal offerings could make a real contribution to public worship. Therefore, we hope our book will find a broader audience in group worship settings.

Five different Annual Conference themes were chosen as division headings for this devotional book. Several scriptures were chosen relating to each theme. Each author or group of authors was asked to prepare a Biblical interpretation; a literary interpretation; a personal experience, reflection or story; a reflection on a Biblical character; a reflection on a historical character; a worship resource; and a prayer. In most instances, the editor has provided the scripture using the Revised Standard Version, an adaptation of that version, or a paraphrase as seemed appropriate. The author or the group of authors is recognized in the table of contents. Individual contributions are also initialed.

The coordinators wish to give grateful acknowledgement to all the women who shared their talents and concerns in the preparation of this book. In addition to those whose contributions are included in the book and named in the table of contents, we would like also to recognize the efforts of the Steering Committee of the Caucus and Shirley Kirkwood, Caucus Worker, for their support and assistance.

The coordinators and the Caucus are indebted to Church Women United and the Fellowship of the Least Coin for a generous grant toward the publication of WOMEN AT THE WELL. According to Grace Nies Fletcher in her book *In Quest of the Least Coin* (Morrow, 1968), the Fellowship of the Least Coin was started by Shanti Solomon, a Christian woman from India who was a member of an International Fellowship Team of Reconciliation formed by the Presbyterian Church to foster Christian forgiveness among people from opposite sides of World War II. As she searched her Bible in the Philippines, she read of the Samaritan who aided Jesus and thought that the women from the villages of India were like the priests who drew away from the problems of the world. Then she read about the widow who gave her two mites and the movement was born. "The widow's mite! That's the answer! You have to give yourself along with your least coin." Women give once a month the "least coin" in their country's currency and themselves. By 1968 they had contributing members or had given assistance in 29 countries. Now they are assisting the Womaen's Caucus of the Church of the Brethren as we try to reach out to Christian women to provide worship materials that recognize the worth and contribution of women. We are deeply grateful, and feel very honored to receive that assistance.

We wish to acknowledge also interest free loans and contributions from many Caucus members and friends which keep the Caucus going and make such projects as this possible.

Betty Jo Buckingham
Jean Lichty Hendricks

All
Creation
Waits

Creation of Humanity

Genesis 2:4b-7, 20-25

In the day that the Creator God made the earth and the heavens, when no plant of the field was yet in the earth and no herb of the field had yet sprung up—for the Creator God had not caused it to rain upon the earth, and there was no human to till the ground; but a mist went up from the earth and watered the whole face of the ground—then the Creator God formed a human of dust from the ground and breathed into the human's nostrils the breath of life and the human became a living being . . . . The human gave names to all the cattle, and to the birds of the air and to every beast of the fields; but for the human there was found no fit helper. So the Creator God caused a deep sleep to fall upon the human, and while the human slept, took one of the human's ribs and closed up its place with flesh; and the rib which the Creator God had taken from the human, God made into a female and brought to the human, now a male. Then the man said, "This at last is bone of my bones and flesh of my flesh; she shall be called Woman because she was taken out of Man."

Therefore a man leaves his father and his mother and cleaves to his wife, and they become one flesh. And the husband and wife were both naked, and were not ashamed.

RSV adapted

Biblical Interpretation

In the second chapter of Genesis God's created living being, known as *'adam* in Hebrew, is placed at the center of creation. The images surrounding *'adam's* creation—a mist that rises to water the whole face of the ground, for example—are cooperative, generative, even procreative ones suggestive of an intrauterine environment. The writer tells us in verses 4b-7 that the body of *'adam* is formed from the dust of this freshly moistened ground (known as *'adamah* in Hebrew) and that God's breath gives life to the body. Flesh and spirit are given life simultaneously, an effect of the Creator's presence and movement within both the earth and all life forms. Just as there is no dichotomy between spirit and flesh implied here, so *'adam* is a unitive human being, not specifically male or female. Until God shapes human and animal forms out of the moist earth and breaths life into them, there is no relationship, only undifferentiated unity.

The writer's intent in vv. 4b-7 and vv. 20-25 is to illustrate the mutual desire and need for relationship between God and the created and among all living creatures. By bringing the animals to *'adam* to be named (v. 20), God asks for *'adam's* assistance in establishing relationship, and thereby God extends participation in the creative-relational process. *'Adam's* naming of the animals is not an act of domination or control but one of stewardly identification which makes relationship with the animals possible.

The writer underscores the importance of relationship in creation when *'adam* and God together discover no one "fit" for *'adam* among all the creatures of the earth. Once again God extends participation in creation to *'adam* by creating two distinct sexual beings—man (*ish*) and woman (*ishsha*)—from the one living being, *'adam*. In this act, God is like a mother-father bringing forth a new form already latent in the flesh of *'adam*. In the distinction of male and female, *'adam's* potential for creativity has become actual power to continue the procreative and relational processes heretofore wholly initiated by God.

The significance of this further creative act is not simply biological; the writer also uses it metaphorically to depict the relationship between the Creator and all human beings. The exclamation *ish* utters to *ishsha* in v. 23 is also God's exclamation to each of us.

Having recognized their inherent unity and mutuality, male and female cleave to one another as God cleaves to us (as close as our very breath) for relationship and continuing expression.

Throughout the entire Genesis 2 passage, God moves *within* all life, not aloof and outside as a construction supervisor. Every creative act of God's lessens God's power *over* life and encourages participation *with* it. By deepening the cooperation between the Creator and the created, the writer reveals God's preference for intimacy and evokes our devotion to God and our reverence for one another.

RKJ, DOW

Literary Interpretation

November Wind

(a lament for Ethiopian children and parents)

You brood around the world with gusts of gray,
And, mixing mottled light and shade, you play
On marigolds now drying on my ground;
You leap o'er leaves, toss milkweed seed to tease
The mother gone to harvest and to store
Against the winter hidden in your breath.
But whipping round the world another way,
Your brooding's neither jest nor dance upon
Fall vegetation firm and nourishing;
Instead you lift and cradle preying birds
That wait upon the empty arms who'd gone
For promises the barren ground couldn't keep.
If you're the breath that suckled us from earth
To life, why now torment us with dry dust?

RKJ

Personal Reflection

Carolyn's call came the morning after Dawn and I had spent several hours in exegetical discussion of Genesis 2. The call—to tell me that her dad had died—brought the images of the Genesis storyteller into living focus.

After a four-year struggle against painful disease, Ross had laid down his energetic vision and practical acts of mercy which had characterized his adult life. But it was not these lively acts that Carolyn wanted to remember as we talked. Instead, she told me of the final hours with her father, hours that pushed aside the veil imposed between physical and spiritual reality.

During the final twenty-four hours of her father's life, Carolyn sat by his bedside bearing silent, and occasionally verbal, witness to her faith in God's presence in and with all creation. When several nurses came to move her father from his left side to his right—an excruciating ordeal for him because of the severe infection of the left side of his face—Carolyn asked if she might remain with him. The nurses invited her not only to remain but also to assist them. Lovingly Carolyn helped to turn the naked, frail form. As she did so she viewed unflinchingly her father's wasted body, even his penis, and thought that except for the seed from his earthly organ she would not have come into being. Cleaving one to another, her mother and father had participated in fashioning a woman who was now reverently attending the passage of the flesh back to the earth.

The process was, of course, highly personal. But it was, as Carolyn said, also cosmic. In this brief moment she realized that the words "bone of my bones and flesh of my flesh" described both her relationship to her father and to humanity. She and Ross had come from the flesh of the earth as members of the family of 'adam, into which God breathes life. This Spirit which animates all life also binds together the physical and the spiritual, female and male, Creator and created.

RKJ

Biblical Characters

Anna and Simeon

No one knows much about the life of the prophetess Anna. Among Bible characters she is relatively reputationless. In Luke 2:36-38 we learn that as an eighty-four-year-old widow she has been filling her nights and days with prayer and fasting. One might assume that such faithful vigil could only have been prompted by one who already senses the presence and activity of God in her own life.

On the day that Simeon comes to the temple longing for consolation of God's relationship with himself and with the people, Anna is ready to receive God's message of salvation. When she hears Simeon's testimony, she gives thanks and proclaims, to all of us still waiting, that God resides in the presence of all people. Simeon and Anna both had longed for the joy and wholeness that relationship with God brings; together they announce their certain consolation to the world.

There are other women and men like Anna and Simeon, known through scripture or forever unnamed to us, who are vehicles of vision and revelation. Jesus used such people often in the parables. A shepherd who sets out after one straggling sheep and a woman who searches hopefully for a silver coin let their longing lead them to that which they have lost. When their search is completed, their joy overflows into celebration, as does God's heart in restoration of relationship with us.

It is the vision of reunion and perserverance in longing that these simple people—an old man, a widow, a shepherd, and a woman in search of her coin—hold up for us. By caring for their trusts and by following their own hearts' longings, they reflect the Creator's care and longing for the created.

RKJ, DOW

Historical Character

Noni

"Whoever does the will of God is my brother, and sister, and mother." Mark 3:35

Noni and I had always been close. For as long as I can remember, my Italian grandmother and I spent most of our Saturdays together singing, cleaning, talking, and preparing pizza for supper later in the day. But of all the words and silences we shared, none was so profound as the experience on our trip to Italy in the summer of 1976. It was at that time that I realized how profound and God-like are the relationships we create and re-create with those we are closest to: relationships that may include yet transcend physical bonds.

During our travels through Italy, Noni and I stayed for several days at the home of relatives who lived in Genoa. I remember vividly the smells of freshly-made bread and grated cheese in the marketplace, the sight of children playing boccia ball along the narrow roadways, the sounds of laughter mixed with political debate in the city streets, and the touch of loving arms as I embraced for the first time many of my family members. There was not a relative who did not welcome me with open arms. But my cousin Bennito's welcome and acceptance I did not understand.

From the beginning, Bennito took an unusual liking to me. He accompanied me wherever I went, even taking time off work to show me the city. As a fourteen-year-old girl I appreciated his help and, of course, enjoyed the attention of a man fifteen years older. I did not at first question his constant attention, although I suspect Noni must have taken note of it.

One evening Noni and her sister wanted to spend some time alone walking through the city. Bennito and I decided to drive through the parkway just outside Genoa. Frequently he stopped the car to talk and then would try to hold my hand or caress me in some way. At fourteen I did not understand what his touches meant. Though this was my cousin, I did not like what he was doing. When he grabbed my arm, I jumped from the car and ran. Confused, I ran quickly at first. But when I found that he was not chasing me, I slowed down and made my way through the city streets back to the apartment. I took the elevator to my aunt's apartment and discovered my cousin sitting inside—alone. He offered no apology as he told me what a special relationship he thought we had. I listened carefully as he closed the apartment door and sat me down beside him on the couch. In only seconds he began again to touch me as I did not want to be touched, imposing himself on me now with force and anger. In confusion and hurt I jerked myself away and leapt toward the door. At the same moment I heard Noni and my aunt just outside. Noni greeted me with a kiss. I was not crying or trembling but was very quiet. Her gentle eyes held me silently for a moment. Then she simply said, "It's late. I'll be with you in the bedroom in just a minute."

I sat on the edge of the large double bed, and a moment later Noni shut the door and sat down beside me. She did not ask me any questions as I sat staring at my hands. Noni glanced at me in silence once or twice. In the dim light I could see reflected in her eyes all the anger, tears, and hurt that I was experiencing. Somehow Noni knew what had happened. When I looked at her I witnessed for the first time the pain that she had experienced in her own life. Her body bore the scars of abuse, and I realized that she, too, had known the confusion and agony of twisted relationships. In this instant she was no longer a seventy-six-year-old lady but became a woman like me and like all other women who have known the tragedy of distorted relationships.

When Noni died this past summer, we still had not discussed what happened that evening in Genoa. We did not need to. Her actions throughout life were prompted by a merciful, unconditional love that not only took away my fear and shame but also freed me to wait for and to expect wholeness in my relationships with others. As I helped to carry her casket at the cemetery, I realized that it was more than my grandmother that I held: she was a sister whose love upheld me that night in Genoa and had transformed our old beings and familial bonds into something more whole and closer to the heart of the Creator.

DOW

Worship Resource

Creation Fable

God created the world and filled it with plants and animals. To tend this lovely garden and these beautiful beasts God created two human beings, one female and one male. For a while the humans lived in harmony, rejoicing in their task of caring for the plants and animals God had created.

But when the female human being became pregnant and bore a child, the male did not understand that he too had a role in this creation story. He became jealous of what he presumed to be the female's ability to create a child alone. Being jealous he told the child this story:

> God created the world and filled it with
> plants and animals. To tend this lovely
> garden and these beautiful beasts, God
> created a male human being . . .

BJB

Prayer

Creator God, you planned a garden full of peace and beauty
We have twisted your design, we have corrupted our relationship
    with each other and with the world.
Creator God, you planned a universe in which we could be
    co-creators
But we have been discontent with sharing that creative power and
    have seized even more power in our own hands
But, O God, you still reach out to us to rebuild the bridges between
    Creator and created. You reach out through the prophets,
    through family members and friends, through Jesus who
    taught us again of your search for union with your creation.
May we turn again to you. May we see again the vision of your
    garden full of peace and beauty. Amen

BJB

May the Unborn Praise God

Psalm 102: 18-22

Let this be recorded for a generation to come, so that a people unborn may praise Yahweh: Yahweh looked down from the holy height, from heaven Yahweh looked at the earth to hear the sighing of the captive, to set free those who were doomed to die; that all people may declare in Zion the name of Yahweh, and in Jerusalem Yahweh's praise, when people gather together, and nations, to worship Yahweh.

RSV adapted

Biblical Interpretation

One hears in this passage both distress and hope. Those who are held captive look forward to their liberation. Yahweh will hear their sighs and act to free them. Then a people yet unborn can gather together to proclaim and praise Yahweh.

This passage is part of a prayer raised to God by the downtrodden during their distress. It includes both personal and collective laments. The psalm begins with a cry that God hear the cry of distress in this prayer. A personal lament follows in which the psalmist vividly describes debilitating illness and a feeling of being forsaken by God. Then a collective lament for a broken Zion and its destitute is raised. Interspersed throughout the psalm is recognition of God as the creator who will endure forever.

Underlying the prayer is awareness of the brokenness which has entered the harmony of God's creation through human sinfulness. The brokenness of Zion—the people God freed from bondage in Egypt and brought to the promised land—is also acknowledged. Yet the psalmist believes that God's creative and liberative activity will continue. Zion will be built up. The captives and those doomed to die will be freed. Children will dwell secure. Then a people yet unborn will come together to praise God!

PB

Literary Interpretation

Hear my cry of distress, O God!
For my heart is heavy
both with my pain
and that of those near me.

We cry out of our brokenness
for wholeness.
We cry out of our captivity
for liberation.
We cry out of our doom
for new life.

We hope against hope
that in this nuclear age
there may yet be
generations to be born
and that they will come together
in praise of you, our Creator!

PB

Personal Reflection

A lament like that of this psalm has often been within my heart. As I have felt my own pain and witnessed the brokenness of the world around me, I have also felt God-forsaken. These feelings have been especially keen since my move to New York City a few years ago.

My marriage ended after several years of painful struggle. Although this decision was made prayerfully and brought feelings of relief and inner peace, there were also times when I felt the pain of a broken relationship. I lament the disruption this has brought into the lives of our children and hope that they will not be too deeply scarred.

As in the psalm, my personal pain is part of the collective pain of my time. As I walk the sidewalks of my neighborhood, I never fail to encounter one of the city's thousands of homeless women and men. From the windows of my apartment I see huge public housing complexes on the edge of Harlem. I know that although these folk are at least sheltered, many of them face lives of despair because of the discrimination they face as poor black and Hispanic people.

I hear the stories of those who come from around the globe to this world capital to plead for their people. From the Middle East, Central America, South Africa, Ethiopia, Korea, India, Peru, and many other places come stories of hunger, oppression, captivity, and death. Where, I wonder, is God?

Yet I see creation witness to God's presence. I hear the testimonies of sisters and brothers from around the globe to God's presence. I experience that presence in my life. We too record our hope—even in our distress—for a generation to come.

PB

20

Biblical Character

Genesis 16:1-16; 21:4-21

Hagar

Hagar is an early biblical figure who laments her captivity and doom. Her story is in part the story of Sarah and both their stories are part of the story of Abraham. Tension between Sarah and Hagar arises in part from the patriarchal context in which they live. Women are subordinate to men. Their acceptance is dependent on their ability to provide male heirs.

As Sarah seems to be barren, she decides to give her maid to Abraham so "that I shall obtain children by her." Hagar conceived. Sarah became angry with Hagar, as she thought Hagar was contemptuous of her. She mistreated Hagar until Hagar fled into the wilderness.

There an angel appeared to Hagar and told her to return and submit to her mistress. She was also told that she would bear a son who would be called Ishmael (God hears), because God had heard her affliction. Her descendants would be many.

Hagar returned and soon bore a son whom she named Ishmael. After she gave birth to Isaac, Sarah became jealous of Ishmael. She did not want the son of a slave woman to be an heir with her son. So she had Abraham banish Hagar and Ishmael into the wilderness. There they soon ran out of water. Hagar cried out that she not see the death of her child from thirst. An angel appeared and showed Hagar a well with water. Hagar's release from captivity seemed to be one that doomed her and her son to death. But her cry of affliction was heard and she and her son were spared death.

For what do we cry out? Do we cry out against loss of privileged status or sharing our wealth as Sarah did? Or are our cries for those who are unjustly enslaved or doomed to death? Do we help perpetuate systems in which some are privileged while others are afflicted? Or do we hope and work for systems which make possible the well-being of all?

PB

Historical Character

Julia Esquival

Julia Esquival cries out for her people through her poetry as did the psalmist. She has seen women, men, and children in her native Guatemala exploited, persecuted, and murdered by the military governments which have ruled since a U.S.-backed coup in 1954 overthrew the country's democratic government. Over half of her people live in extreme poverty while two percent of farm families own eighty percent of the country's farm land. Most of this land is used to grow food for export rather than to feed the people of Guatemala. Those who challenge this system are repressed and persecuted.

Julia lives in exile. She speaks, writes, and organizes on behalf of her people. She is sustained in this work through her deep faith and hope in Jesus Christ. For Jesus too experienced oppression and persecution. Jesus is present even now with people in their oppression and persecution. And in Christ there is hope for liberation.

Julia's poem "Confession" expresses both her despair and hope.

> How many times
> did I wish to close my ears
> to your voice,
> to harden my heart,
> to seal my lips,
> to forget forever
> the pain of the persecuted,
> the helplessness of the outcast,
> and the agony of the tortured,
> but your pain
> was my own
> and your love
> burned in my heart! . . .
>
> I have brought
> my cause before you,
> and I know that you will free
> the flesh of the poor

from the hand of the oppressor.
As a brave warrior
you defend the cause
of the persecuted,
and open up paths for us
in the darkness,

You illuminate our darkness
and fill our sadness
with hope.

We need not fear facing sadness in our lives and the life of the world, because we too can be filled with hope if we open our hearts to the pain and love of those with whom Jesus suffers. We can join our voices with Julia's in crying out for an end to this oppression. Will I open my heart and raise my voice with her?

PB

Worship Resource

Call to Confession and Commitment

ONE: There is One who is present with humanity even in our deepest pain and despair. We are called to come to that One and confess our suffering and sin.

ALL: In the midst of our pain, Holy One, we sometimes doubt your presence. We close our hearts to you. We want to open them but are sometimes afraid that the suffering of the world will overwhelm us.

ONE: Christ will be present with us in our sufferings. Christ will bear the pain with us. We will bear the pain together. And from the pain will come hope.

ALL: We open our hearts . . . . We feel the suffering of those who are oppressed in many places . . . . We confess that we sometimes benefit from systems which oppress others . . . . Forgive us, thou who hearest

23

our affliction. . . . Empower us to lift our voices against oppression and injustice.

PB

Prayer

May Julia Esquival's "Confession" be ours:

> Captivate me . . . [God].
> Till the last of my days,
> wring out my heart
> with your hands
> of a wise old Indian,
> so that I will not forget
> your Justice
> nor cease proclaiming
> the urgent need
> for humankind
> to live in harmony.
> Amen.

PB

Creation Awaits
With Longing

Romans 8:18-23

I consider that the sufferings of this present time are not worth comparing with the glory that is to be revealed to us. For the creation waits with eager longing for the revealing of the children of God; for the creation was subjected to futility, not of its own will but by the will of God who subjected it in hope; because the creation itself will be set free from its bondage to decay and obtain the glorious liberty of the children of God. We know that the whole creation has been groaning in travail together until now; and not only the creation, but we ourselves, who have the first fruits of the Spirit, groan inwardly as we wait for adoption as children, the redemption of our bodies.

RSV adapted

Biblical Interpretation

In this passage of Paul's letter to the Romans Paul continues the discussion of what Christianity is (the author's basic task in the entire book) and moves to consider faith as it relates to the entire created universe. Paul says that even as the followers of Jesus suffer, so the entire creation suffers, as a woman in childbirth, as it waits for the final freedom and splendor to be revealed at the end of time when sin and death will be no more. However, that suffering does not begin to compare with the splendor which is promised in the new age.

This passage leads us to think of the creation story in Genesis 2. The disobedience of Adam and Eve reverberated in all of creation—the ground was cursed and humankind and nature became, in a sense, adversaries instead of partners. The sin of humankind results in the entire physical environment being cursed, and woman, man and nature are "in travail." No longer is the earth an idyllic garden, where everything is good. Instead, woman will bring forth children in pain, and man will struggle to exist on land choked with weeds.

Paul sees the work of Christ as changing all of this. The whole universe waits eagerly for God's children to be revealed, for then the original harmonious relationships intended by God will be restored. This is the splendor which is promised. Until then, the universe groans.

DW

Literary Interpretation

From Eve and Adam's time
It's been a struggle,
Female/male; humanity/nature.
Toiling, grinding, pushing, pulling.

When we become new beings
The struggle continues.
But it is the struggle to be in dialogue,
The struggle to care rather than to possess,
To nourish rather than to destroy.

At that final day
A shout will go up
From the dandelions and the redwoods.
The lion and the lamb
Will frolic together.
And God will again create the New Garden,
The Peaceable Dominion.

DW

Personal Reflection

This scripture reminds us of the "already—not-yetness" character of our lives as children of God. At times, when the Spirit touches us, we have small intimations of the splendor about which Paul speaks. Perhaps it comes as a sense of oneness that we feel with another person or a group of persons. Perhaps it is felt when we are overwhelmed by the beauty of a landscape, or the exquisiteness of a single flower. It may even come when we celebrate the life of one we mourn. At these times we know that *already* God is present, at work, doing a new thing.

Unfortunately, most of the time the *not-yetness* is the dominant theme in our lives. We spend so much life energy on our own selfish concerns that we are not open to the fact that God is already present in the creation and in our neighbor. So it is that we struggle—we sense that a new creation is waiting to come into being, but we cannot seem to acknowledge that it is God who gives the birth.

Is this tension the reason for our groaning, and for the groaning of all creation? We *know*, yet we do *not* know. We love, yet we do not love. It is within this tension that we live. In this passage, Paul does not describe a Utopia. Rather, a vision of redemption is promised. And it is this vision which is our hope and, therefore, our empowerment.

When we are true to this vision, our relationship to creation becomes one of partnership rather than dominion; one of responsibility rather than right; one of care-giving rather than exploitation. Then it is that we realize that the community of God encompasses women, men, nature and God.

DW

Biblical Characters

The Role of Women in the Bible and the Church

It would appear that the passage in Romans 8:18-23 which speaks of the groaning of the whole created universe also speaks of something which is uniquely understood by women. As a part of the created universe women know, perhaps better than anyone, the frustration, the longing, of waiting for God to bring in the new age.

Women in the Old Testament are most often portrayed as inferior beings. There are, of course, women who at times achieve great moral influence, for example, Miriam, Deborah or Huldah. But more frequently women are seen as subordinate to men, symbolic of sin and evil, and are regarded as the property of their husbands and the bearers of sons. Sometimes they are unnamed, and the tales told about them, as Phyllis Trible notes, often turn out to be "texts of terror."

With the coming of Jesus, there is a remarkable change. Jesus talks with women, heals them, and numbers them as followers and friends. Jesus treats them with respect, as persons in their own right, and in doing this, breaks down yet another barrier among the Jews of that day. Jesus holds a long conversation with a Samaritan woman. Jesus' feet are washed by a woman's tears. Jesus visits with Mary and Martha. And women are the first to know of the resurrection.

The early church, as described in Acts, continues to incorporate women into its life in important ways. But something happened as the years went by, and by the third century A.D. the patriarchal system was in place once again. From then until now women have known not only the pain of childbirth but the pain of being considered less than full human beings in society and in the church.

So women can really resonate with Paul who says that "even we, to whom the Spirit is given as first fruits of the harvest to come, are groaning inwardly while we wait for God to make us daughters and set our whole body free." Our identity as children of God has been made clear in Christ, and we are very thankful. But women groan inwardly and wait for this to be affirmed in the church and in society, so we can be truly free to nourish and care for the earth.

DW

Historical Character

Dorothy Sayers

Dorothy Leigh Sayers is probably best known in the United States as a British writer of mystery stories, many of which feature amateur detective Lord Peter Wimsey. Many Christians first came to know her through her radio play on the life of Christ, entitled *The Man Born To Be King*, published in 1943. But she was also an early Christian feminist of extraordinary creative ability. She was one of the first women to be granted degrees from Oxford University and maintained scholarly interests all through her life, even while earning her living by writing advertising copy for a large agency in London.

Sayers grew up as an only child in a vicar's household. Very early on she was impressed with the down-to-earthness of the people with their foibles and their pain, as contrasted with the solid verities of the faith. She developed a theology early in life. She particularly liked the image of God as Creator, and saw persons as creative by nature, even as God is. As a writer, this was important to her.

In many ways Sayers' life was difficult. She was not blessed with good looks or the usual social graces. Her marriage, though it held together, was not a very compatible one. But her creative mind, her excellent sense of humor, and her ability to see life realistically and in its totality, were her strengths. Most importantly, she sought always to see the relationship of her faith to all of life, human and non-human. The interdependence of all of God's creation, held together by Love Incarnate, was proclaimed by Dorothy L. Sayers in her writing as well as her life. She saw herself always as a fallen child of God, but, because she allowed Christ to become incarnate in her life, she became a vehicle of the love of God in the world.

Is this not the way we are to live in this interim period, as we wait for "the splendour to be revealed?" Only if we do will our groaning in travail be redemptive.

DW

Worship Resource

Litany

For the beauty of the landscape
For the beauty of the leaves of fall and the blossoms of spring
For the beauty of the faces of your children around the world

WE PRAISE YOU, O GOD, THE EARTH IS YOURS!

For the majesty of the mountains and the serenity of the hills
For the clear flow of the rivers and the steady pounding of the waves upon the shore
For the plants and animals which surround us and sustain us

WE PRAISE YOU, O GOD, THE EARTH IS YOURS!

For the joy of seeing, and singing, and speaking
For the joy of loving and being loved
For the joy of nourishing and caring for each other and for the earth
WE PRAISE YOU, O GOD, THE EARTH IS YOURS!

DW

Prayer

O God,
Forgive us our lack of sensitivity to all the marvelous beauty of your creation.
Forgive us when we misuse your gifts;
  When we cover the earth with black-top and ticky-tacky boxes;
  When we rape the forests and the soil and the mines;
  When we pollute the air and the water and the ground;
  When we act as if we are the owners of the earth instead of your guests;
  When we fail to share with those in need.

Help us to remember our interconnections with all that is past, all that is now, and all that is to come.
Keep us aware
  that on this earth we have no continuing city;
  that we are but pilgrims on a journey;
  and that we must not destroy what sustains us,
  Lest those who follow us are deprived of the beauty and abundance we have enjoyed.

May we express the freedom we know in Christ in ways that encourage hope and justice and peace to flourish in your world.
Amen.

DW

Creation Is Good

1 Timothy 4:1-5

Now the spirit expressly says that in later times some will depart from the faith by giving heed to deceitful spirits and doctrines of demons, through the pretensions of liars whose consciences are seared, who forbid marriage and enjoin abstinence from foods which God created to be received with thanksgiving by those who believe and know the truth. For everything created by God is good, and nothing is to be rejected if it is received with thanksgiving; for then it is consecrated by the word of God and power.

RSV

Biblical Interpretation

This text consists of a brief portion of Paul's letter to a dear friend and assistant, Timothy. This letter was probably written in response to conditions in the Church—especially in the locality of Ephesus—which threatened the Church from without and from within. Most heretics were teaching doctrines which were based on the belief that the body and all forms of matter were entirely evil and only the spirit was altogether good. Many persons who believed such heresies sought destruction rather than resurrection of their bodies, while others used such false teachings to justify immoral behavior. Paul speaks clearly through Timothy to people during that time and to us today who would believe doctrines which contradict Christianity. When we see the term faith in this passage, it emerges with a new meaning which assumes that Christianity consists of a well-defined body of teaching.

This passage begins with a prophecy which the author believed was being fulfilled at that time. We understand from the text that in later days some Christians will depart from the faith by paying attention to seducing, deceitful spirits which lead them astray with their doctrines. Those spirits work through people who are habitual liars with seared consciences and who are unable to recognize the truth. Just as a part of the body can lose its feeling when there is an injury to the central nervous system, likewise the conscience can become dulled when seared as by a hot iron so that it can no longer function as an inward monitor. As we comprehend the impact and consequence of a seared conscience, we can relate better to Christians who are often blind to injustices, e.g., the destructive nature and repercussions of racism, sexism, materialism, militarism, etc. Paul shows us that true faith and a sensitive conscience work together so that the Christian understands that one does not serve God by becoming a slave to rules and regulations. Christians serve God by believing in the goodness of all of God's creation, accepting God's gifts with thanksgiving, praying that God will awaken our consciences in dulled areas, and sharing God's gifts with others.

BC

Literary Interpretation

God, our Creator, creates day by day
   Making for us what is good:
All that sustains us without and within,
   Like our daily water and food.

We must not yield to the words of deceivers,
   Whose hearts are wicked and hard;
For they teach that we must reject
   Certain gifts created for us by God.

They do not seem to understand
    That God's gifts are ours to share,
Because all things made by God are good
    When received with thanksgiving and prayer.

Let us rejoice and be glad in our hearts
    And in song our voices raise,
For God, the creator of heaven and earth,
    Is worthy of honor and praise.

                                                    BC

Personal Reflection

I believe most people in our society would verbally affirm that they believe everything created by God is good. Yet, it is difficult to understand how most of those same people support governmental policies and priorities which focus on war rather than global issues and humanity. Our legislators continually approve budgets with increased allocations for military expenditures and decreased allocations for humanitarian concerns. Although some may feel uncomfortable with my use of the word "support," I think we show our affirmation and support for governmental decisions when we fail to inform our decision makers of our beliefs and values.

We frequently discuss our attitudes with friends and family, but we procrastinate when we plan to let the president, a legislator, governor or other elected officials know our feelings about pending legislation or decisions which impact policies. I believe we are concerned about the threat of nuclear annihilation, U.S. support of South Africa and its apartheid regime, U.S. intervention in Central America, our reaction to "terrorism," global problems related to water, food, torture, oppression, etc. I believe we care about the impact of budget cuts in domestic social programs, the rising unemployment in cities and foreclosures on farms, the increase in the numbers of "street" people, drug dealers and users, and other urban and rural problems. Unless we are speaking out against these kinds of issues and working toward solutions, we are a part of the problem. Silence can be deadly.

Because we are Christians and believe in the goodness of God's creation, let us pray that God will enable us to be better stewards of all that God has created.

BC

Biblical Character

Luke 10:30, 31

The Priest

In the book of Luke, Jesus teaches a powerful lesson on the meaning of "neighbor" in the familiar parable of the good Samaritan. Usually when the story is told, the role of the Samaritan is emphasized, but I have chosen the priest as the character to focus on here.

When Jesus told this story, it was probably easier for the scribe to comprehend the scenario and the actions of the priest than for us today. The road from Jerusalem to Jericho was well-known as a dangerous road with many sudden turns and hiding places for robbers. Consequently, the circumstances and events described were commonplace happenings at that time. Although I was surprised when I first heard the story that the priest was not the one who immediately offered aid to the half-dead man, Jesus' listeners no doubt knew the risk the priest must consider in such an encounter.

The scribe and the priest were, no doubt, knowledgeable of the law. They knew that it was written in Numbers 19:11 that a priest who touched a dead person was unclean for seven days. Although the priest did not know whether or not the victim encountered was dead, he knew the penalty for touching a deceased person. He would lose his turn of duty in the Temple. The priest probably valued human life and would have willingly affirmed verbally that everything created by God is good. Yet, when faced with a situation where he had to decide between ceremony and charity, he hastened on. For him the risk was too great. The Temple and its liturgy meant more to him than a part of God's wonderful creation.

Let us not condemn the priest but seek out those portions of our own consciences which may be seared so that we do not decide as the priest did when meeting the challenges of our own day.

BC

Historical Character

Mattie Cunningham Dolby

Mattie Cunningham was born in Indiana on October 28, 1878 and lived to be 78 years old. She is noteworthy for the quality of her life and the Christian commitment she exemplified by her witness, words and deeds. She was a missionary, a Brethren minister, and servant of Christ who unfortunately suffered the pain of racism throughout her existence because God created her black. Although it is not written, it is apparent that such pain was even more severe when its ugly roots crept into the Church which she so dearly loved.

When she was 26 years old, she went to Palestine, Arkansas with Elder James May and his wife to work with the black people there. Elder May's wife died shortly after their arrival, and May returned to Ohio, leaving Mattie to work alone with the few black Brethren whom he had baptized. She worked diligently to fulfill her responsibilities for about three years when illness forced her to return home also. While she was in Arkansas, her faith increased as she labored to bring liberation through Christ, and education, to her downtrodden and neglected race. She wrote several intuitive, prophetic, and challenging articles which were published in *The Missionary Visitor*. Her writings contain such valuable lessons and insights that they should be republished and disseminated throughout the denomination to enlighten and enrich people today.

Mattie married Newton Dolby, a Baptist minister, in 1907. He soon became Brethren, and they were installed as deacons later that same year. Their marriage was blessed with six children, and the Church was blessed by their commitment and service. They worked with a small group in Jeffersonville which was under the auspices of the Frankfort, Ohio church. Mattie's special talents and abilities were so visible that she was called to the ministry and installed with a "laying of hands ceremony" on December 30, 1911.

She was an innovator in many ways. She was: the first black student to attend Manchester College; the first female to be installed as a minister in the Church of the Brethren (this historic action was accomplished by a Negro Brethren congregation in Frankfort, Ohio); and the first black woman to contribute articles to a Brethren publication. Unfortunately, she was also probably the first Brethren minister to be invited by a church of that denomination to worship somewhere else. Mattie and her family willingly commuted many miles to worship regularly in the Springfield, Ohio Church until they were no longer welcome there. Mattie remained steadfast in her faith and continued to serve the Church in another denomination for the remainder of her life.

Because of the magnitude of her contributions, the depth of her commitment, the rich legacy of her writings, and for numerous other reasons, it is impossible to do more than give a glimpse of Mattie Dolby here. She served God, studied God's word, taught and preached the Gospel, and shared God's love generously. Her life is definitely representative of the goodness of God's creation.

BC

Worship Resource

Litany of Thanks

Leader: We praise you, O God, for your greatness and the magnificence of your creation.

People: O God, we thank you for all that you have created.

Leader: We praise you, O God, for the food which you have provided to sustain and nourish our bodies.

People: O God, we thank you for the food we have eaten.

Leader: We praise you, O God, for your indwelling spirit which empowers and enables us to be your disciples.

People: O God, we thank you for your continual presence within us.

Leader: We rejoice in your love, O God. A love so great that you gave your child so that we might be saved and reconciled to you.

People: O God, we thank you for your constant love.

Leader: We praise you, O God, and rejoice in the love we share with our parents, spouses, children and friends.

People: O God, we thank you for the love we receive from our families and friends.

Leader: We praise you, O God, for the goodness of your creation and the abundance of your blessings.

People: All creatures give you thanks, O God, and revere your holy name. For you alone deserve such honor and praise. Amen.

BC

Prayer

O God, our creator, we thank you for all your bountiful blessings and the magnificence of all your creation. We know that you have made us in your image and created us and all things well. Yet, because you gave us minds to reason and freedom of choice, we are constantly making poor decisions which lead us away from you and your will for us. Help us to be reconciled to you through Christ.

O God, our parent, we come seeking guidance and strength to yield to your will and to respond to the call of the Gospel. We realize that we cannot complete even the most simple tasks well without you. Help us to love you and each other so that we may be able to work together to overcome the barriers of racism and sexism which divide us. We ask that you would enable us to proclaim the Good News of our Savior, Jesus Christ, rather than to boast of our own goodness.

O God, Almighty, help us to be good stewards of your love and to share our faith in word and deed. We know that we have portions of our consciences which are asleep, and we beseech you to awaken us in those areas so that we may work together to free the oppressed, to respond to those in need, and to be peacemakers in our day. We know that you can strengthen and enable us to be followers in the ways of Jesus because you are all powerful.

We come rejoicing in the knowledge that you have told us to ask, and we will receive; to seek, and we will find; to knock and the door will be opened to us. O God, we come asking, seeking and knocking in the name of Jesus.

Amen.

BC

Partakers
of the
Promise

And Sarah Laughed:
Women of Good Humor

Genesis 18:9-15

God's messengers said to Abraham, "Where is Sarah your wife?" And he said, "She is in the tent." God said, "I will surely return to you in the spring, and Sarah your wife will have a son." And Sarah was listening at the tent door behind him. Now Abraham and Sarah were old, advanced in age; it had ceased to be with Sarah after the manner of women. So Sarah laughed to herself, saying, "After I have grown old and my husband is old, shall I have pleasure?" God said to Abraham, "Why did Sarah laugh, and say, 'Shall I indeed bear a child, now that I am old?' Is anything too wonderful for God? At the appointed time I will return to you, in the spring, and Sarah shall have a son." But Sarah denied, saying, "I did not laugh," for she was afraid. God said, "No, but you did laugh."

RSV adapted

Biblical Interpretation

Genesis 18:9-15 is a delightful little story tucked into the middle of the saga of Abraham, the Patriarch of Israel. A little story? It is, indeed, the tip of an iceberg, so to speak, in that it points to religions and cultures that are possibly four millenia old. And it pictures a woman who spent most of her life in Mamre, a terebinth grove, a sacred place in ancient Canaan. The important events of Sarah's life were connected with that sacred shrine, and it is there that she is buried.

It is likely that Sarah was born in a city state on the Euphrates River, Ur of the Chaldees, present-day Iraq. She has often been presented as a jealous, headstrong woman who banished Hagar out of anger. Rather, she probably was a priestess who acted with authority out of her own tradition. She was a devoutly religious woman of high rank, guided by ordinances referred to as the Code of Hammurabi, a legal system applicable in her homeland. In the foreign land of Canaan, she was "struggling to maintain the social traditions to which she was accustomed, traditions she had brought with her from Mesopotamia," according to Savina J. Teubal in *Sarah the Priestess*. The Genesis stories, declares Teubal, contain elements that are not typical of the patriarchal system of Canaan. A non-patriarchal system flourished at that time, with some very important differences in social customs and traditions. Descent was through the female line. Kinship was determined through the mother's bloodline, so that her marriage to Abraham was legitimate. Succession was by the youngest rather than the oldest. A man was required in marriage to leave his place of birth and live with his wife's relatives. Sisters could marry the same man.

Religion permeated the lives of Ancient Near East peoples. The office of priestess was one of many religious functionaries. One restriction common to those offices was that those women were forbidden to have children, although some were allowed to be married. Sarah and Rachel both speak of providing themselves with heirs— suggesting the Mesopotamian culture of matrilineal descent.

It is clear that the matriarchs were very influential in the lives of their children and their husbands. In Genesis 21:12, God says to Abraham, "Whatever Sarah tells you, do as she says." Sarah was following Mesopotamian law in her banishment of Hagar. Abraham's comment, "Deal with her as *you* think right" is a recognition of Sarah's authority.

To be a priestess in Sarah's day meant that the woman was the Goddess incarnate. One of her functions was to participate in the Sacred Marriage, upon which the welfare of the whole community depended. In the name of the Goddess, she received the bridegroom (priest-King) in order to bestow fertility on the land and the people. This may explain Sarah's sexual activity with the kings, Pharaoh and Abimelech. Her story in Genesis points to the presence of a social system that was non-patriarchal, struggling against being swallowed up by the patriarchal system in the Land of Canaan. Sarah tried to "hold the line" against a male culture that eventually relegated women to a position of subordination and outright oppression. Her banishment of Ishmael was an effort to insure the continuance of her own traditions through Isaac. Ishmael represented Egyptian culture and religious rites, one of which was circumcision, a foreign practice which was undoubtedly unacceptable to Sarah. As a religious woman, she was intensely concerned over the religious life of Isaac. So, she took aggressive action to remove this foreign influence over him. And her action was supported by Abraham, evidence that she was a woman who was highly respected by the men in her life. Sarah gives us a vision of a non-patriarchal society where women are religious leaders with important contributions to make to their life and times.

To understand Sarah's laughter, we need to look at two Hebrew words: YSHOEL and AKARA. YSHOEL means Isaac, the name she would give her child. The word means, "May God smile" or "God has smiled." Sarah's laughter may be an allusion to Isaac's name. The word AKARA, is always translated as "barren," which seems to imply that divine intervention was needed for the conception to occur. It has another meaning as well which has almost been lost— childless. Childlessness implies a *choice* on the part of the woman. It is highly likely that a woman of Sarah's religious stature made a choice. Could it be that she laughed at the announcement of her pregnancy because she knew it already? In any case, Sarah knew a good joke when she saw one. She was no victim. She took centerstage with her laughter. And she said, "Everyone who hears will laugh with me."

BG-R

Literary Interpretation

And Sarah Laughed

To laugh is to create a world.
Sarah laughed.
Having chosen as priestess not to bear a
  child,
Now in old age she laughs
At the incongruity of her pregnancy, her
  secret.
She laughs because of the promise
Of new life and laughter in the world
Coming through her.
Miracle upon miracle.
She would bear a child.
And Sarah laughed.

Women of the world laugh as they weep in
  their struggle.
Life does overcome death.

BG-R

Personal Reflection

The Power of Laughter

Sarah and Rachel, women of Ancient Near East Mesopotamia, and Sojourner Truth, daughter of a Dutch slave and Mau Mau Bett, form an unlikely trio. Their lives were quite disparate. However, they had much in common. They were women. They lived in changing times. They were intent on dealing with the issues that confronted them in their daily living. They were profoundly religious. They were compelling authority figures. And, they were skilled in using humor. They give to us women in our day the precious legacy of laughter.

When Sarah learned that she was to bear a child in her old age, she laughed. As Rachel sat on her camel with the stolen household gods beneath her, she was poking fun at the cultural image of women being unclean during menstruation. When a man interrupted a speech Sojourner Truth was giving in 1850 with, "Do you really think all your talk is accomplishing anything? I don't care for your talk any more than I do for a flea!" she countered the insult with humor. Without missing a beat, she replied: "Perhaps not, but it'll keep you scratching." Yes, indeed, these three forebears of ours were women of good humor.

There is an old adage that says, "Laughter is the best medicine." Indeed, to be able to laugh is to heal. A woman said to me recently, as she was dealing with a particularly sexist and oppressive system: "So long as one woman can laugh, we are not completely under the domination of fear or anxiety." Sarah's laughter was a recognition of incongruity. Rachel's laughter was a sign of courage. Sojourner Truth's laughter was an assertion of dignity. In all three cases, laughter made the situation manageable. It got things in perspective. Because laughter is social, it forms a bond among like-minded people. Simultaneously it draws a line which establishes distance. Laughter is a paradox: while it defies authorities and defines boundaries between ourselves and another, it endears us to people on our own terms. It taps the wild in us. It keeps us from taking ourselves too seriously. It produces a sense of exhiliration, perhaps defiance. Laughter gives us power, a sense of taking control. If I can mock what hurts me, as Rachel did, I begin to claim the reality of my own perceptions.

Laughter forms bonds and creates solidarity. Sisters, let us laugh together.

BG-R

Biblical Character
based on Genesis Chs. 29-35

Rachel

There are striking similarities between the stories of Rachel and Sarah. Rachel, also, was born in Mesopotamia and brought with her to Canaan the customs and traditions of a non-patriarchal social system. She, too, lived by the Code of Hammurabi. She, too, was probably a priestess, a religious woman of great respect. In her theft of the household gods, she has been presented as a scheming, conniving, hostile woman. Not so. She had every right to the symbols of her position, especially after her father's behavior toward herself, her sister and her husband.

Rachel's introduction into the Old Testament is hidden in the story of Jacob's journey to Paddan-Aram following his theft of the blessing from Esau. The story is replete with details of the human condition—greed and self-seeking, manipulation, jealousy, one-upping tactics, deceit and trickery. It also demonstrates the human capacity for love and committed relationships between people, creation and God.

Rachel is introduced into the story as Jacob's kinswoman, the daughter of his mother's brother Laban, the Aramaean. She appears first as a shepherd in the distance, coming toward a well in the fields of Mesopotamia outside Haran. Jacob had arrived there after his long journey and is pictured conversing with the shepherds whose flocks lie nearby. As they meet, Jacob removes the stone from the well single-handed, waters the flock, kisses Rachel and weeps aloud. Rachel then runs to her father, who comes to meet Jacob and embraces him as one of the family. Then follows the story of the long years of Jacob's love for Rachel and his service to Laban to acquire Rachel and Leah as wives.

The names given to Rachel (Ewe) and Leah (Wild Cow) are titles of Mesopotamian goddesses. Ninsuna, "Lady of the Wild Cows," and Duttur, the personified ewe, were revered by cowherds and shepherds along the Euphrates River according to Thorkild Jacobsen writing in *The Treasures of Darkness*. This heightens the contrast between Rachel as a religious woman of great respect and

47

reverence, and Laban, the crafty and deceitful tyrant. The word used for daughters, *banoth*, in Hebrew is quite similar to *bonoth*, the word for builders. The Jewish Midrash (*Midrash Rabbah*, Soncino Press, 1951) claims that this likeness is meant to say that it was from these daughters that the world was built up.

In the story of the departure of Jacob from Laban, Rachel is the star. In Genesis 31:19, a succinct and pointed verse, Rachel takes action. The verse reads: "Laban had gone to shear his sheep, and Rachel stole her father's household gods." Thereon hangs a tale. Shearing was a busy time and everyone was preoccupied with both the work of shearing and the preparation of the feast to follow it. It was a well-chosen time for Rachel's action and the subsequent departure of Jacob's household from Laban. It points to the fact that matriarchal power was operative in decisive ways for Jacob, as it was for Isaac, his father. The image of Rebekah's involvement in the stealing of the birthright for Jacob is set over against Rachel's stealing of the household gods of her father. In both cases, the patriarchal power base was upset by women. As Rebekah became an intermediary between Isaac and God in her successful abortion of his intention to make Esau the bearer of the blessing, so Rachel's theft and subsequent relinquishing of Laban's household gods assured for Jacob his place in the patriarchal structure of the Israelite people. In both cases, the "guilty one" became the bearer of the promise. The Midrash asserts that "Rachel's theft was a noble one."

The Elohist story of the pursuit of Rachel, Leah and Jacob by Laban and his kinsmen is at once exciting, dangerous and humorous. Rachel's tent was pitched along with the others in the hill country of Gilead, supposedly a seven-day journey from Haran. Laban confronts Jacob regarding his secret departure and the theft of his gods. He dramatizes the importance of the theft of the gods and demands a reason. Jacob, unaware that Rachel is the thief, responds to Laban's urgency by declaring the death penalty on the one in whose possession the gods are found. There follows a ludicrous scene: the frantic, funny, fruitless searching by Laban of one tent after another. When the search is almost completed, Rachel appears, contained and poised, sitting complacently on her camel. She has tucked the household gods into the saddle litter and is sitting on them. Secure in the knowledge that she is in complete control of the situation, she is calm, composed and free of fear.

With utter complacency and decorum, assuming absolute innocence, she says to her father: "Let not my Lord be angry that I cannot rise before you, for the way of women is upon me." She had defiled the gods, and Laban could not come near her, or he, too, would be unclean. He is foiled. Rachel is clearly in power. The covenant which follows is significant in that it marks their peaceful break with each other and Jacob's complete turn toward Canaan.

Rachel was a woman of good humor. She was politically astute. She trusted her own perceptions and was true to her own religious experience. She took the cultural restrictions and expectations her society placed on her and used them to achieve her purposes. She took daring action in relation to existing options in her situation. Viewed from this perspective, Rachel, the loved, becomes Rachel, the lover. Rachel, the beautiful, becomes Rachel, the defiant. Rachel, the instrument of men, becomes Rachel, the agent of Truth. Rachel, the insignificant wife of a patriarch, becomes Rachel, the matriarch whose choices directed the destiny of her people.

BG-R

Historical Character

Sojourner Truth

She was named Isabella Bett when she was born into her black people in 1797. She bore intolerable and brutal treatment as a slave child and young woman. The horrors she and her family endured put fire into her bones. At age 46, she told a friend, "The Lord has given me a new name—Sojourner. I'm to travel up and down the land, telling people about God's commands. God has work for me to do ahead, bringing the truth to people. Truth—my name will be Sojourner Truth." (Helen Peterson, *Sojourner Truth, Fearless Crusader*, Garrard, 1972).

She was a tall woman of dignity and self-assurance, the first black woman to give anti-slavery lectures in America. She knew who she was. She knew the truth on which she stood. She spoke eloquently and fearlessly for her people. Her very first lecture, she began by singing:

> I am pleading for my people,
> A poor, downtrodden race,
> Who dwell in freedom's boasted land
> With no abiding place.

Her experience as a champion for the cause of blacks and women earned for her harassment and disrespect. She was never without a quick and spicy response. In Ohio in 1851 a law student hurled at her the words, "Negroes are fit only to be slaves. If any show intelligence, it's because they have white blood." She rose to her full height, held her head high and responded, "I am pure African. You can all see that plain enough. None of your white blood runs in my veins." (Dale Spender, *Women of Ideas*, Rutledge and Kegan Paul, 1982, 267). During another lecture, in response to the men who were claiming that women had no rights because Christ wasn't a woman, she said in a loud voice: "Whar did your Christ come from? From God and a woman, that's who. Man had nothin' to do wid him." (Spender, 265).

In 1852 at the Women's Rights Convention in Akron, Ohio, she was incensed at a minister's angry comment: "God did not intend women to have equality with men!" She rose and gave her famous speech:

> That man over there say that a woman needs to be helped into carriages, and lifted over ditches, and to have the best place everywhere. Nobody ever helped me into carriages or over mud puddles, or gives me a best place—and ain't I a woman? Look at me. Look at my arm! I have plowed and planted and gathered into barns, and no man could head me—and ain't I a woman? I could work as much and eat as much as a man when I could get it, and bear the lash as well—and ain't I a woman? I have borned thirteen children and seen them most all sold off into slavery. And when I cried out with a mother's grief, none but Jesus heard me—and ain't I a woman? (Spender, 268)

Sojourner Truth visited Abraham Lincoln and Andrew Johnson in the White House, appealing to them to address the plight of the freed slaves. She took a paper to Congress requesting land in the west for the "empty-handed colored people for all their unpaid labor." A senator responded, "Congress will do what the majority of American's demand." Quick as a flash, she responded, "Then I shall go and stir up the majority!" She was 73 years old at the time.

What a woman of humor she was! She died at 86 in Battle Creek, Michigan. Her words still ring in our ears:

> If de first woman God ever made was strong enough to turn the world upside down all alone, dese women togedder ought to be able to turn it back and get it right side up again. And now dey is asking to do it, de men better let 'em (Spender, 269).

BG-R

Worship Resource

Litany: So Let Us Laugh Together

One: The laughter of Sarah, Rachel and Sojourner Truth reaches us across the ages.
All: Our laughter will roll back to blend with theirs.
One: Their laughter put things in their proper perspective.
Two: Their laughter drew boundaries between themselves and others.
Three: Their laughter bonds us in a common understanding.
Four: Their laughter builds in us a sense of solidarity with them.
One: They laughed through their struggles.
All: So will we.
One: Sarah laughed at the incongruity of her life.
All: And so will we.
One: Rachel laughed as a sign of courage.
All: We will laugh with courage, too.
One: Sojourner Truth laughed as an assertion of her dignity.
All: We will laugh our oppressors into silence.
One: And ALL the sisters say
All: So let us laugh together.

BG-R

Prayer

Spirit of courage, dignity and joy,
Fill us with laughter.
Create in us that strong womanspirit
That arises out of vulnerability linked with humor.
Let the voice of laughter resound within us
In powerful bonding and sisterhood.

So may our lives be blessed with strength and courage.
So may we be the bearers of Hope
To those who weep.

So be it.

BG-R

I Will Take You
For My People

Exodus 6:2-7

And God said to Moses, "I am Yahweh. I appeared to Abraham, to Isaac, and to Jacob as God Almighty, but by my name Yahweh I did not make myself known to them. I also established my covenant with them to give them the land of Canaan, the land in which they dwelt as sojourners. Moreover, I have heard the groaning of the people of Israel whom the Egyptians hold in bondage and I have remembered my covenant. Say therefore to the people of Israel, 'I am Yahweh, and I will bring you out from under the burdens of the Egyptians, and I will deliver you from their bondage, and I will redeem you with an outstretched arm and with great acts of judgment, and I will take you for my people, and I will be your God; and you shall know that I am Yahweh, your God who has brought you out from under the burdens of the Egyptians.'"

RSV adapted

Biblical Interpretation

In these verses, Moses is told to recount to a group of Hebrew slaves that their God, Yahweh, promises to deliver them. This is one of several formulations in the scriptures of God's covenant with Israel. Each account stresses certain elements of the agreement.

This instance falls many years after the promise to Abraham (Gen. 12:1-3) and a short time before the great covenant events at Sinai when the laws for living in community were given.

Note that this is a covenant between a stronger and a weaker party. (Such covenants existed between rulers and their subjects, for example.) But in this case, the stronger party does not present demands and the weaker party make promises, as would be expected. Rather, the stronger party, Yahweh, promises to deliver the people from their bondage and be their God. Yahweh will do this because, "I have heard your groanings, and I promised the land to your forebears." In response, Israel has only to consent to be Yahweh's people, i.e., to accept in faith the covenant Yahweh offers. God's covenant rests on God's grace.

In this particular situation, however, it is not easy for Israel to accept in faith that Yahweh will free them and give them a homeland. When Moses receives this message, faith was anything but easy. Moses and Aaron had already had an audience with Pharaoh and presented Yahweh's wishes. The result, however, was that their oppression increased. Straw was no longer provided for the bricks they were required to make. Any meager faith they had mustered, any shimmer of hope that Moses' words of Yahweh's promises had ignited, faltered when Moses' brave actions resulted in worsening conditions.

So the people came complaining to Moses, "Now look what you've done!"

Moses, in turn, confronted Yahweh, "Look, I did what *you* said, and what happened? Things got worse, that's what! And now everybody's mad at me."

In answer, Moses is told, "Say to the people of Israel, 'I am Yahweh and I will bring you out from under the burdens of the Egyptians.'" God offers no other argument than to remind them who they are, the people of Israel (not a nameless group of slaves); and who it is who promises, Yahweh.

Needless to say, that was not enough for the people just then (verse 9). They, like the Egyptians, had to be convinced by the events that followed, before they were willing to venture out of their captivity into an unknown freedom where the only thing they knew was that Yahweh had pledged to be their God.

LL

Literary Interpretation

First Day at School

A child and a stranger,
Fearful and trembling,
Tearful, in turmoil,
Shunned and excluded,
Separate, desolate.

Strange faces, strange whispers,
Strange whispering laughter.

Cruel bondage of shyness,
Cruel shyness of weeping.

With an outstretched arm
She caught me
And I was comforted.
With a strong hand
She smoothed my hair
And I was not afraid.

With an outstretched arm
And a strong hand,
She led me into
My new land.

HHA

Personal Reflection

Covenant—God's Promise as Model for Families

Each of us has felt something of both the promise and the challenge of the covenant relationship described in Exodus 6:2-9 through the family experiences of our lives. When I've reflected on my birth family, I recall expectations (and unspoken promises) of relationships between my parents and me; acceptance came through laughter and tears, work and play; as well as the times of distance, tension and growing—all the while, caring and knowing we were "family" and that within the relationship we were "one people," however flawed we each might be. And so we each come to some understanding of the religious significance relating us to the larger human family.

It's been through my experience of a blended family that I've been enabled to expand my vision for and responsibility to the promise of covenant. Our family (which united two families changed by divorce and death) presented a variety of exciting, frustrating, demanding and often seemingly impossible obstacles to ever becoming "one family." When Jim and I married in 1973, there were many hopes and countless unknowns as we began life together with our five children (my daughters, 13, 10 and 8 years old, his daughter and son, 12 and 14 years old) in a house new to all of us, in a community and school new to four of us, with new and different relationships for all seven of us. How does one realize and create God's covenant in this setting? I often asked. Initially, I expected or naively believed that good will and dreams alone would establish the promises of covenant and create a sense of family under that one roof. Now, looking back over our journey through that "wilderness" of unknowns where we worked on relationships, established trust (necessary before concern about behavior and appearances, although there's a real tension here), I feel intensely the meaning and significance of this Scripture, knowing how easy it is to disbelieve because of everyday experiences of failure and disappointment.

Today there are those special times when a note is found on a windshield as a child spots the car at a mutual favorite mountain site, step-siblings help each other move into their own "homes," holidays and birthdays are remembered and celebrated jointly, phone calls exchange the highs and lows between different members—these are relationships born of a promise to be a family, to be "one family"—different backgrounds, heritages, genes, and habits, yet united. I know that if we as a united woman and man can recreate this promise from a less than perfect set of circumstances, then what harmony and oneness can God create in the global family!

Dare we believe and covenant to be delivered from our bondage, to be redeemed, to be one people?

SK

Biblical Character

(based on Gen. 17:7; Ex. 6:2-8; I Sam. 18, 19, 25; II Sam. 3, 5, 6)

Michal

From the beginning women have heard in their inmost being the universal call from their Creator: "I am your God! You are parties to my Covenant and blessing!" But, blocked by age-old interpretations and fears, they have remained outside the Covenant promises, falsely labeled "For men only!"

Michal was a daughter of the tragic King Saul who had broken the holy Covenant and missed his high destiny. The brief record shows her as resourceful and independent but used as a pawn in the deadly rivalry of her father and David, her betrothed. She planned a successful escape for her new husband from the embittered King. For punishment her father passed her like a chattel to another man whose devotion she won and whose children she probably bore.

But in time that first husband of a few days, now King David, jealous for his lost royal property, ordered her torn from her weeping husband to add to his other wives and concubines. What life she had with these strangers in the crowded women's quarters is not known. But surely she had much to suffer, ponder, and endure.

Then one day, from a window, she saw David in religious frenzy leaping, somersaulting, and dancing before the advancing Ark of the Covenant, clad in a scanty loin cloth and attended by shouting men and screaming women. She waited for his return and went to meet him, not bowed to the ground in the expected obsequious woman's posture, but upright and face to face. And she rebuked him scornfully for behavior unbecoming to a king. Her punishment: immediate separation and a mandate of childlessness to her grave.

This was her moment of truth in action—from female to male as responsible co-inheritors of the Covenant and its obligations. The scribes have belittled and obscured the import of her daring judgment.

There have always been Michals—rising to act on an inner revealed truth, their brave, beautiful, or thoughtful achievements devalued, misappropriated, misinterpreted, prevented or blotted from the record. Yet from the beginning the Creator has had a covenant with them—as with each one of us: "And I will establish my Covenant between me and you and your descendants after you in their generations as a perpetual Covenant to be God to you and your descendants . . . ."

We have the word of the Most High that the groanings have been heard, we have the promise of the Most High to bring us out from under burdens, to deliver us from bondage, and to redeem us with an outstretched arm and with great acts of judgment—the word that we too, with our brothers, are called: "I will take you to me for a people! I will be your God!" Let us then listen for that word—learn, know, and claim that word—get up and respond with joy to that word as proud and responsible women of the Covenant.

GP

Historical Character

Naomi West—Angel

As an underclasswoman at Bridgewater College my acquaintance with Naomi E. Miller, an upperclasswoman, was understandably limited since there were three Naomi Millers on campus and all in the same class. However, I soon learned to associate the one called Naomi "E" with lovely black curly hair and dark expressive eyes. Naomi "E" was never destined to stand in someone else's shadow.

After several years of high school teaching, she married the Reverend Guy West, a well-known evangelist and pastor in the Church of the Brethren. Together they served in pastorates in Virginia, Pennsylvania and later in California. She was not merely a helpmeet to Guy, but she was Naomi "E," intelligent, creative, willing to serve tirelessly and always ready to challenge others. Wherever they ministered, from the east coast to the west, Naomi actively worked for peace and justice, promoted projects to provide better housing and food for the needy, coached drama groups and helped provide sanctuary for servicemen turned CO. Even in supposed retirement there are few idle moments. She carries a heavy load of church duties and ministers to those in Bridgewater Retirement Home.

One of her major efforts has been in behalf of refugees in the aftermaths of World War II and the Vietnam War. Again Naomi's efforts were directed to the homeless. There were Bakhtiar and Kamaran, Quan and Hung Troung (Quan's new baby was named Naomi S. W. Troung), the Nguyen Family of 11 members, Asmaret, Araya and countless others. The empathy shown to these seems only a continuation of her concern for the women and children in the Bowery to whom she administered while Guy was doing clinical studies in New York.

The following incident speaks volumes about Naomi. Once, while Naomi was on her knees bandaging an open sore on the leg of one of the many refugees who spent time in the West home, the refugee looked down at her and said, "You are an angel!"

Yes, Naomi is an angel—not an antiseptic one, but an earthy one who literally binds the wounds and washes the feet of the world. She extends God's covenant to all people, ". . . You are no longer strangers and sojourners but you are fellow citizens . . ." in a strange land.

EPG

Worship Resource

Partakers of the Promise, Based on Exodus 6:2-7

Voice 1: I am Yahweh,
I Am Who I Am.
I appeared unto Eve and Adam;
"Don't eat, don't touch."
"This ground is holy."

Voice 2: I appeared unto Abraham and Sarah:
"Walk before me and be blameless."
"I will bless you, and I will multiply your descendants."

Voice 3: I appeared unto Isaac and Rebecca:
"Dwell in the land which I tell you."
"I will be with you, and I will bless you."

Voice 4: I appeared unto Jacob:
"Israel shall be your name."
"I am God almighty; a nation shall come from you."

Voice 1: I appeared unto Moses:
"I am your forebears' God."
("Have you eaten of the tree?")

"I've seen my people suffer."
("The ground is cursed for you.")

"I hear my people cry."
("I'll multiply your pain.")

"I've come with an outstretched arm for you."
("I drove them East of Eden.")

Voice 2: I will take you for my people, and I will be your God and you shall know that I am the Creator your God.

All: God, you have always been our home. Before you created the hills or brought the world into being, you were eternally God and will be God forever.

Let us your servants, see your mighty deeds; let our descendants see your glorious might.

God, may your blessings be with us.

PJ

60

Prayer

Creator and Spirit within each of us, sometimes I feel I've had a glimmer of the vision of your covenant for the human family and what it might be in a land where we are not strangers to each other. Yet it's not easy to imagine myself in this land—mostly because I think about my own family circle with its loyalties and possessions, or my denomination and the politics of the church, even. I feel the bondage of a clean house and caring well for "my" family, working for appearances or the preservation of customs and habits. God, I know and feel that our lives are narrow and that our living does not include the whole of your family; that our bondage keeps us from believing in and fulfilling our part of your promise to create this family of all people. We don't know how to weave together the many threads of family living in covenant relationships.

I see your spirit within those I learn to know whose lives I share as a volunteer. I see your spirit in all who experience pain and the loss of life; I feel the oneness of the human family through shared grief. I feel your spirit in the tears and anger of parents who cannot agree on anything except their love for their children. My faith in your promise is restored as I recognize your presence in that pain and suffering in the world. I often have not recognized it as your spirit working through my life in those most difficult hours; that spirit that is the source of both pain and joy—I've wanted the promise without the pain of change and rebirth.

Teach me to be a listener; to pay attention to your creative spirit within my life and others, to use pain and anger rather than deny or belittle it; to grow toward the fulfillment of your covenant with all the human family. Let me hold my "helpful answers," give up my bondage to human systems that provide easy and possessive answers in order that other questions can be asked—that your unique promises may be revealed anew in the lives of each member of this family. Help me to envision your promise each day; enable me to live out of this larger perspective.

SK

How Can I Give You Up, O Ephraim?

Hosea 11: 1-9

1. When the people of Israel were children, I loved them. I called my children out of Egypt, 2. but the more I called, the further they went from me; they made sacrifices to the Baalim and burned offerings before images of gods. 3. I was the one who taught the children how to walk, who held them in my arms; 4. but they were unaware it was I who healed them; they did not realize that I had lifted them to support them like little children, that I had fed them when they were young. 5. They shall go back to Egypt, the Assyrian shall be their ruler; for they have not turned back to me. 6. Slashing swords shall be swung over their blood-spattered altars, shall do away with their babbling priests, 7. and shall destroy my people in return for their schemings, stubborn as they are for continuing with them. Though they call on their high god, even then that god will not restore them to their previous position. 8. Is there any way I can give you up, Ephraim? Could I turn my back on you, Israel? How can I make you like Admah or treat you as Zeboyim? My heart is changed already and I am sorry for what I said. 9. I will not let loose my anger, I will not act to destroy Ephraim; for I am God and not a human being, the Holy One in your midst.

Paraphrase, CB

Biblical Interpretation

The Bible often uses human love to portray God's love. In this passage of Hosea, the love of a parent for a child is used to show the depth of God's love. Israel is pictured as God's first-born, called to be God's representative to the world but bound to run off to the neighbors "parents" rather than heeding God.

God's love is demonstrated in terms more familiar to women in that day and this. God taught Ephraim to walk. Ephraim was cradled in God's arms, healed of illness by God without realizing it, led and fed by God.

The people of Israel suffer because they turn away from their heavenly parent, but God cannot forget or destroy Ephraim. Instead God will restore the people to their homes after their punishment, despite their faithlessness.

BJB

Literary Interpretation

Echo Pantomime of Hosea 11: 1-9

Introduction: Hosea wrote about the people of Israel as if they were children and God was their parent. Let's pretend we are each a child of Israel. We will act out the story as it is told by Hosea. I will say a few words and do some actions, and then you will say and do the same, like an echo.

Words	Actions
When I was a child in Israel	Point to self
God loved me	Cross arms on chest
God called me out of Egypt	Hold hand behind one ear, as if listening
But the more God called	Hold hand behind other ear
The further I went from God	Take 2 steps backward
I made sacrifices to Baal	Extend arms outward in front

And burned offerings before images of gods	Raise arms to protect self from heat of the fire
God taught me to walk	Step in place 4 times
God held me in tender arms	Pretend to hold a baby
But I did not know	Shake head "no"
It was God taking care of me	Cross arms on chest
I did not know	Shake head "no"
God had lifted me up	Hold arms up in the air
I did not know	Shake head "no"
God had fed me	Pretend to put food in mouth
I must go back to Egypt	Slap thighs as if marching
Assyria will be my ruler	Place crown on "another" head
For I did not turn back to God	Look down
. . . But then God said	Look up
Is there any way I can give you up?	Extend arms out in welcome
Could I turn my back on you?	Turn body to left
God's heart was changed!	Clap hands 3 times
God still loved me	Cross arms on chest
God's anger was not let loose	Shake fists and then change to a "gentle" handclasp
For God is God	Extend arms out in welcome
And not a human being	Point to self
God still loves me!	Cross arms on chest

CB

Personal Reflection

Watching parents with a newborn child usually conjures up reminders of the dreams I had for each of my two daughters when they were born. Even before they were born I was trying to find out as much as I could about parenting, both in terms of the physical care they would need and the emotional well-being I wanted to provide. Talking with friends who were somewhat experienced as parents, and reading recommended books were the two main sources on which I relied for guidance. I wanted to be the best parent I could be. I wanted to give my children every opportunity and advantage I could. I wanted to offer them the promise of a happy and secure life.

Time passed for me and the reality of parenting was a part of my life. As with most other parents, times of disappointment and frustration were mixed with the promises and rewards of parenting. I have done and said things to my children I never wanted to do or say. Yet they love me still. They have caused negative feelings in me, yet I love them still. Just as the love between my children and me remains, so the love remained constant between the people of Israel and God. God wanted every opportunity and advantage for the people. They had been a special focus on God's energies and had every reason to turn out in the very best way possible, but they turned away and disappointed God.

We, as parents, teachers, or friends have such a short time to nurture and to care for our children. It seems almost inappropriate for us to lose patience with ourselves and with our young friends. Yet lose patience we do! We experience setbacks, disappointments, adjustments. Yet we try not to give up. Parents and teachers will try new techniques, different strategies to help children learn and mature. How can we ever give up hope with a child we recognize as a child of God? Love, hope and the promise are always there.

CB

Biblical Character

The Parable of the Prodigal Son

In the Parable of the Prodigal Son (Luke 15: 11-32) we again read a story in which a child turns away from a parent. The younger son asks for his share of the property. Another way to refer to the property would be to see it as a promise. The younger child had knowledge of the property promised to him. In the same way, the people of Israel had knowledge of the promises made to them by God through their ancestors. The prodigal child wanted to partake of the promise. When the share was given, the child left home.

After squandering all the money, he realized the true wealth he had was with a parent who loved him. He returned home, ready to work as a servant, to admit he had done foolish things. The people of Israel, in the time of Hosea's writing, had experienced the promises of God, but they consistently leaned away from God and spent their time doing foolish things. Surely punishment would come from God. Instead, God's love remained constant!

The love of the parent figure in the Parable of the Prodigal Son is also constant. As soon as the father sees the child returning, he prepares to welcome him with open arms. In spite of the foolishness of the child's actions, the parent is there to provide comfort and support. Not all human parents and children can claim the same relationship. In spite of the faithlessness of the people of Israel, of us as Christians, God is there to be a constant source of security and renewal for us. The promise is there for us to partake.

CB

Historical Character

The Forgiving Mother

It seems likely that it was the father in the story of the "Prodigal Son" who was really prodigal—prodigal with his love. It is hard to identify a historical mother who could be called a prodigal mother, perhaps because there are so many of them. So the story of this unnamed, but very real, prodigal mother is the story of many such mothers as they reach out in forgiveness and acceptance to their daughters and sons.

She was the baby of the family and in a hurry to grow up. He was an older divorced man with several children, the youngest just a baby. They ran away to get married before she was out of high school. The glamour soon wore off as she struggled to care for his children, to make ready to have her own child, and to make a home for a husband who was less and less present and less and less responsible.

So she turned to her mother. And her mother helped her. Her mother did not allow her daughter to take over her parents' home and totally disrupt their lives. But her mother provided a place for her daughter's family to live and baby sat with the children, despite her own full time job and busy household schedule. This allowed the daughter to work part time to provide some financial stability for her step children and her own child.

Then the husband left for good and the daughter invited another man into her home and bed. And the mother continued to "sit" for her daughter's child and to provide a place for them to live.

It is hard in our society to separate doormats from forgiving parents. Many would see the mother in the former role. But unforgiving parents sever relations with their children. Parents who set up strict conditions for their love and forgiveness may turn their children into doormats or may further alienate them.

Forgiving parents run the risk of being abused and misused, but they keep the doors of communication open so their children can come to seek forgiveness. Forgiving parents may need to practice "tough love" but the emphasis must be on love and forgiveness or their rebels may never return. That is the kind of forgiving parent God is.

BJB

Worship Resource

Litany of Confession

Cong.: We come to you, God, aware of the week just passed, feeling a need to confess . . .

Lead.: We thank you, God, for keeping your promise . . .

Cong.: We complain about our neighbors, sometimes our friends, even our family members. They sometimes take time from us we would rather spend in other ways . . .

Lead.: We thank you, God, for keeping your promise . . .

Cong.: We go through some days with no thoughts of you, of how we could serve you; too busy with our world of cares and worries, we forget about the Source of our being . . .

Lead.: We thank you, God, for keeping your promise . . .

Cong.: We ignore those we see who are in need, those who want to talk, to know someone cares, to feel a hand of comfort or support . . .

Lead.: We thank you, God, for keeping your promise . . .

Cong.: We fail to send the letter that is long overdue, to mail the card that is sure to cheer, to make the phone call that would only take minutes out of our day . . .

Lead.: We thank you, God, for keeping your promise . . .

Cong.: We turn away from what we once knew was dear to us; there are moments when we feel faithless . . .

Lead.: We thank you, God, for keeping your promise . . . for loving us still!

CB

Prayer

We come to you, Creator God, with thanks for the covenant you have made with your people. You have promised us that we can be your daughters. Like a mother who cares for her children, you have cared for us, holding onto us when we needed your protection, letting go of us when we needed to try something on our own. We can be excited because we experience a sense of hope, we believe the talents you have given us can be used to make changes, and we even, at times, have the joy of seeing some of the growth beginning to happen.

There are times when we get tired, though, when the struggle seems too difficult, when we experience backward steps which seem to outweigh the forward steps. We ask you to uphold us, God, to give us renewed strength and hope, to give us energy. Feed us as you fed your children in the desert. Sustain us with the reminder that your love is constant and your promises are always there for us to partake.

Allow us to catch a glimpse of those promises. Allow us to catch a glimpse of the vision of freedom and wholeness you would have for all human beings. Enable us to be aware that the great transformation taking place is for the good of all people. Comfort us as we search for life, deliver us from fear and dependence, support us in our thirst for wholeness, give us determination.

Confront us with the responsibility of being called to the promotion of justice. We are called to name the promises of the abundant life. Awaken us to the needs of others, sensitize us to those we see every day, as well as to those we may never see face to face. We need to be filled and refilled with the spirit of your love. Keep us alive with the source and nourishment of your constant love, and fill us with a passionate desire to overcome the obstacles which cause empty and wasted lives. We trust you as our eternal source of energy and eagerly await the fulfillment of our visions. Amen.

CB

God's Promise Has Not Failed

Romans 9:6-12

But it is not as though the word of God had failed. For not all who are descended from Israel belong to Israel, and not all are children of Abraham because they are his descendants; but "Through Isaac shall your descendants be named." This means that it is not the children of the flesh who are the children of God, but the children of the promise are reckoned as descendants. For this is what the promise said, "About this time I will return and Sarah shall have a son." And not only so, but also when Rebecca had conceived children by one man, our forefather Isaac, though they were not yet born and had done nothing either good or bad, in order that God's purpose of election might continue, not because of works but because of God's call, she was told, "The elder will serve the younger." As it is written, "Jacob I loved, but Esau I hated."

RSV, adapted

Biblical Interpretation

This scripture passage is a reassurance that even when a rational view of people and events leads one to conclude that God's promise, "the word of God," has failed, in fact God's purposes can be and are being fulfilled in unexpected ways which we may not understand.

Paul deals in this passage with the problem of the Jews, God's chosen people, refusing to accept Jesus Christ as Messiah. This rejection of God's saving gift seemed to be evidence that God's promise had failed. If God's chosen people refuse to accept Christ, how can God's promise to the patriarchs be fulfilled?

Paul points out that God chose some, but not all, of Abraham's descendants to fulfill the promise. Isaac but not Ishmael, Jacob but not Esau were selected by God for special favor. We do not know why. God works in ways we do not understand. Paul suggests that the Gentiles' acceptance of Christ's salvation makes them "children of the promise." The actual descendants of Abraham, the "children of the flesh," are not necessarily chosen to fulfill the promise.

God's sovereignty gives freedom to choose and to act in ways contrary to our human expectations. Control is still in God's hands, in spite of our failure to understand. Just because things do not happen as we wish them to, as seems "right" and "fair," we cannot conclude that God's promise has failed. Life is not fair. But God is still in charge.

God's ways are mysterious, startling, different: to send a saviour and messiah, and have that saviour crucified rather than crowned! Out of that contradiction, that failure in the eyes of the world, comes Christ's triumph over death, and our salvation. Out of our failures can also come triumph, and the fulfillment of God's promise.

MK

Literary Interpretation

Morning

The sun comes up,
Lighting our darkness,
Warming us with its brightness,
Promising a new day.

Clouds may hide it,
And darkness may come with a storm,
Yet the promise is fulfilled.
At evening,
When the sun sets,
The darkness does not mean
The promise has been broken.
We rest through the dark night
Knowing God is faithful.
The sun will come up tomorrow
Bringing a new day.

MK

Personal Reflection

"This is not the way it is supposed to be." Sometimes I look at my life and echo those words, feeling the deep pain of broken promises and unfulfilled hopes.

When I was young, I met a man and fell in love. We were married, and I expected that we would live happily ever after, as all the story books promised when I was a child. Yet after our two children were born, my husband decided to seek his future elsewhere, with someone else. In my grief, I felt that not only his promise but life's promises to me were irretrievably broken.

Two friends of mine were married and looked forward eagerly to having children. When their first child was born, she was found to be suffering from some kind of brain damage. As they love and care for their severely retarded daughter and struggle to make difficult decisions about her future, it must seem to these parents that their expectations of having healthy, normal children have been bitterly and inexplicably betrayed.

In these situations and others like them, it is tempting to accuse God of somehow breaking the promise we expected to be fulfilled.

After all, isn't God in charge? "Where were you, God? How could you let this terrible thing happen?" we cry out of our despair.

In our humanness, we struggle to understand that which cannot be understood. God is larger than our understanding. Our faith is built on a Saviour who was put to death in a most painful and degrading way, yet through that death God's promise was fulfilled. Which of us would have planned it that way? Even Jesus had a hard time accepting the plan. Is it any wonder, then, that we have difficulty accepting the many different kinds of death, the broken promises in our lives? Yet out of them can come resurrection and new life.

MK

Biblical Character

Based on Luke 7:11-15

The Widow of Nain

The widow of Nain, whose son Jesus raised from the dead in Luke 7:11-15, is a woman we know from our own lives, rather than from the text. The gospel writer tells us only that she was a widow whose only son, a young man, had died.

Those who work with the grieving tell us that the most difficult deaths for loved ones to accept are the untimely, "out of order" deaths of young people. We expect our children to outlive us and live long, full lives of their own. When the promise of childhood and youth is cut short, the pain of loss is very great. At those times, God's promise seems to be irretrievably broken.

The widow of Nain was overcome with this grief, the loss of her only child. Jesus felt compassion for her, and spoke to her, saying, "Do not weep." He commanded her son to arise, literally brought him back to life. The young man spoke, "and Jesus gave him back to his mother."

How we wish such a miracle would happen in our own lives when the pain of loss overcomes us! Doctors are able to miraculously heal many people, but when a person is lying in a coffin, as was this widow's son, no miracle of modern medicine can bring back life. How, then are we to understand?

Perhaps we will never fully understand. Certainly we cannot experience Jesus' compassion first-hand in the concrete way the widow did. But we know that God cares for us in our grief. Death is not the breaking of God's promise, but rather, through Jesus, death ultimately became the means of fulfilling the promise of resurrection and new life. Through our faith, we are offered hope that sustains us, like Jesus' healing touch, in our darkest hours.

MK

Historical Character

Mother Teresa

Mother Teresa has been ministering to the destitute and dying since 1948, when she felt the call to live and serve God among the "poorest of the poor" in Calcutta, India. Her work is with those society has rejected, primarily abandoned children and the dying. They are taken in off the streets and given shelter, food, and care.

The suffering with which Mother Teresa comes into daily contact does not cause her to question God's goodness or to see God's promises as broken. Instead, Mother Teresa sees these bleak situations as opportunities to fulfill the promise of Christ's love. She challenges others also to embody the selfless love that reaches out to those in need.

The question Mother Teresa's work suggests is not whether God's promises have failed, but whether we are failing to help fulfill God's promises. As the popular saying goes, are we part of the problem or part of the solution? Are we preoccupied with our own wounds, or do we reach out with God's healing love? Are we "stuck" in disappointment at what seems to be broken promises to us, or are we about the business of helping to fulfill the promise of Christ's love?

MK

Worship Resource

A Litany For Difficult Days

One: When we feel the despair that comes from broken promises in our lives,

All: WE REMEMBER, O GOD, THAT YOUR PROMISES DO NOT FAIL.

One: When we feel the loneliness that comes from a sense of failure and rejection,

All: WE REMEMBER, O GOD, THAT YOUR LOVE IS SURE AND UNCHANGING.

One: When people and events in our lives seem frighteningly out of control,

All: WE REMEMBER, O GOD, THAT ALL THINGS ARE UNDER YOUR CONTROL.

One: When we do not understand the reasons for the difficulties we face,

All: WE FEEL CONFIDENT, O GOD, IN YOUR DIVINE WISDOM. WE PRAISE YOU AND THANK YOU THAT YOUR PROMISES, YOUR LOVE, AND YOUR POWER SUSTAIN US EVEN IN THE MOST PAINFUL TIMES. THROUGH CHRIST OUR SAVIOR WE PRAY. AMEN

MK

Prayer

O God, I am a woman. Give me confidence in the strength you built into my body and mind before I was born. Help me to rejoice in the knowledge that I am your child, with many gifts given to me from your loving, creative spirit. Teach me your will for my life, so that in my words and actions I may fulfill your purposes.

O God, I am divorced. Help me to know that in spite of failure and rejection, your love for me is sure and unchanging. Even when I feel unacceptable to myself, let me live with the assurance that you still accept me. Help me to give up my need to have things turn out as I have decided they should, and give me the grace to accept what comes.

O God, when I feel overwhelmed with despair because of broken promises in my life, help me to have faith that your promises will never be broken. Give me confidence that your plans, though I do not understand them, are better and larger and are being carried out even in the midst of my own shattered plans. Touch me and heal me, O God, and turn my tears into new hope for the future. Amen.

MK

Covenant: Neither Jew nor Greek, Male Nor Female

Galatians 3: 23-29

Now before faith came, we were confined under the law, kept under restraint until faith should be revealed. So that the law was our custodian until Christ came, that we might be justified by faith. But now that faith has come, we are no longer under a custodian; for in Christ Jesus you are all children of God, through faith. For as many of you as were baptized into Christ have put on Christ. There is neither Jew nor Greek, there is neither slave nor free, there is neither male nor female; for you are all one in Christ Jesus. And if you are Christ's then you are Sarah and Abraham's offspring, heirs according to the promise.

RSV adapted

Biblical Interpretation

Covenant

In the concluding passages of the third chapter of Galatians Paul speaks out with authority concerning justification by faith.

It was a new idea for a new time. This covenant was not laid down by law. It was manifested through the love and sacrifice of Jesus Christ. Through our faith we become heirs to the promise wrought in the new covenant.

One of the striking evidences of the "long way we have come" is the inclusiveness of both male and female in contemporary writing. As a response to the demand for that to happen, this scripture (3:28) is often quoted. For it is Paul saying, "on the other hand" there may be a greater truth than I have yet spoken. It is the same Paul, who apparently admonished women to be quiet in church, to be subject to their husbands, to occupy a secondary role, who speaks to us, but his message is altered.

The good news of the new covenant is that all stereotypes are shattered, all exterior judgments give way under the power of Christ. Then appear those marvelous, insightful words that resonate in the heart of anyone who has ever felt excluded or rejected by reason of ethnic differences, of economic differences, or of differences of sex.

There is a body shift, an "aha!" as the freeing power of inclusive language settles around us.

"There is neither Jew nor Greek, there is neither slave nor free, there is neither male nor female: for you are all one in Christ Jesus." Hallelujah!

PH

Literary Interpretation

"Paul, you almost
did us in . . .
You decided for us . . .
our silence in the sanctuary
our absence from the realm of influence
our subjection to the men-folk
(Even subjection in love
is subjection!)

But you came around . . .
Under the influence of
greater light you spoke for us . . .
In Christ there is neither
male nor female.

How we resonate to your proclamation.
Thank you for noting what
we women always knew.
You've come a long way, brother Paul!"

PH

Personal Reflection

I have been there . . . in front of the all-male board, hearing them quote freely from Paul's words but always steering clear of Galatians 3:28.

For many years I felt called to proclaim God's word as a freelancer, unaffirmed and unblessed by the church. But the moment came when I desired with my whole being to claim that blessing. All the miles traversed, the churches and meeting rooms visited . . . all those times I went in God's name to share my faith . . . wanted response.

When the moment of testing came, my prayer was that I shed no tear; for if one tear rolled down my plump cheek, I could be immediately classified as a hyper-emotional female unfit to minister in God's name.

The questions flew at me—not questions of discernment concerning my faith or my ministry—questions of why . . . questions of motivation ("jealous of your husband?" one preacher asked). "Why" questions always imply judgment. After a long series of such questions, I had used up a lot of my arsenal of answers. One more "Why?" was the proverbial last straw. I waited silently and then I heard myself saying, "Gentlemen, I enjoy the priestly role." Their response was a long silence.

To whom did the priestly bailiwick belong?

I found it interesting. Did they forget the Brethren do not claim priests? Did they forget Galatians 3:28: "In Christ there is no male nor female?"

PH

Biblical Characters

based on Luke 10: 38ff; John 11:1-12:2

Mary and Martha of Bethany

Two sisters were special friends of Jesus. Their home, the home of Mary and Martha, was open to Jesus, and it was a place where holy hospitality, love and comfort abode. The sisters both loved Jesus . . . it was not only the radiance and charisma of Christ's personality that drew them. Jesus had raised their brother Lazarus from the dead . . . it is hard to show enough gratitude for such a gift.

On this day, on the way to Jerusalem, Jesus stopped at Bethany to see these friends. It would be a time of physical refreshment and psychological uplift, for Mary and Martha's devotion was obvious.

The visit turned into a small drama as a rather clumsy situation developed between the two sisters. There is a vivid picture of Mary sitting at Jesus' feet, listening with a divine attentiveness. Poor Martha is out in the kitchen rattling the pots and pans, but Mary has no ear for her cry for help. In exasperation Martha rushes in and says, "Listen, Jesus, don't you even care that my sister has left me to do all the work alone? And if you do care, tell her to get herself busy."

And Jesus' answer, which is a dart in the heart to every woman who has ever stood at a hot stove, was, "Martha, don't be so uptight: don't try to do so much. You are upset about too many things . . . there is only one really necessary thing: Mary has chosen that and it shall not be taken away from her."

Life is ambiguous . . . we are forced into being Marthas and we are drawn into a great desire to sit at Jesus' feet and share that "best part which no one can take away from us." The "Mary and Martha syndrome" continues, but more and more women are taking advantage of numerous opportunities to participate in prayer groups and in spiritual life formation. The number of women ministers in the Church of the Brethren steadily increases and more women are attending seminary than ever before. We cannot turn our backs on the Martha in each of us, but more and more we can claim the Mary and choose the "better part."

PH

Historical Character

Florence Allshorn

At a crucial time in my own journey some thirty years ago, the writings and biography of an obscure English mystic came into my hands. Her witness has been of singular import to me personally, and to thousands of others who knew her or read her very small but significant written contributions.

Though Florence, who lived from 1887 to 1950, had nothing the world said she should have so that happiness might attend her, her life did shine with the light of the indwelling Christ and the joy that is inherent in Jesus' continual presence. Florence was an Anglican missionary to Uganda. When her health failed, she returned to England and taught young women who were preparing for the mission field. She built a retreat center, St. Julian's, where weary pilgrims could be refreshed spiritually. Her only written guide for her life was the two great commandments. Her writing reflects her insight concerning love as a way of life.

Those who knew her best speak of

a strange and delightful contradiction in her personality. She was at once gay and yet profoundly serious around her gaiety. She appreciated and offered the best of material pleasures and comforts and beauties and yet one suspected that they really meant nothing to her. She looked ready to share one's most trivial or sordid experience and one knew she would be untouched by it at the same time as bearing it. She gave the impression of toughness and delicacy, like silver wire.

Perhaps that is a description of saintliness.

Florence Allshorn taught me a beautiful lesson in words that lasted longer than her pilgrimage did. Florence said, "Whenever you look at anyone, see them as Christ wants them to be." And I do look closely at friends and strangers, watching for Christ's intent for them. But I have looked more closely at myself to see if weakness and unworthiness can become strength and worthiness in Christ's eyes.

PH

Worship Resource

All One in Christ

Call to worship: This is the day that God has made. Let us rejoice
and be glad in it. Let us rejoice because God has shared life
with us in the presence of Jesus of Nazareth and the Holy
Spirit. Let us be glad that this revelation frees us from the
bondage of ethnic differences, economic differences and
sexual differences.

Scripture: Galatians 3:23-29

Hymn: "All are One in Christ," (Available in *Come Sisters, Celebrate and Sing* and *Come Sisters, Break Forth and Sing*, 1977 and 1978 Church of the Brethren Women's Conference song books. From *Because We Are One People* song book published by Ecumenical Women's Centers, c1974.

Litany:

One: All of you who were baptized in Christ have clothed yourselves with Christ. In Christ there is neither Jew nor Greek.

All: In Christ we are one—the color of skin, the difference of language, the rules of culture cannot separate those who love Jesus.

One: In Christ there is neither slave nor free.

All: In Christ we are all set free from whatever has been our chains; the bonds of slavery fall away, melted by Christ's love for each of us.

One: In Christ there is neither male nor female.

All: Those who belong to Christ are people of grace, people who live with loving hearts unfettered by sexual inequality.

One: You are all one in Christ Jesus, heirs according to promise.

All: Thank you, God . . . All Praise be to God . . . Hallelujah!

Hymn: "Come, People, Celebrate and Sing," *Brethren Song Book*, No. 88

Benediction: May you leave this place free of any bondage that time, culture, and society have placed upon you. May you share your freedom in Christ with all you meet, generous with Love and Grace to all of God's children.

PH

Prayer

Our Gracious God, the Great Reality of our lives, to you we bring our deep hurts, our pains, our anger, and our pettiness. Through your loving kindness lift those burdens that throw shadows on our ability to love others as you have loved us.

Thank you for our roots, for the heritage of strength passed on from the myriad women who came before us. Our history is a history of loving and serving you with courage.

Thank you for the deep insights expressed in those words, "In Christ there is neither . . . male nor female." Thank you for freeing each of us to become what you want us to be. Grant us the quietness and reflective time to discern your will in our lives. Grant us the courage and strength and commitment to live toward that vision.

Empower all those in the leadership of the church to graciously use their gifts which came from you, to help those who are faltering along the way. Help each of our sisters to name and claim their gifts, and to use them always for your glory.

In Jesus name. Amen.

PH

God's Grace
as Gift

On Finding Favor With God

Exodus 33:12-19

Moses said to God, "See, thou sayest to me, 'Bring up this people,' but thou hast not let me know whom thou wilt send with me. Yet thou hast said, 'I know you by name, and you have also found favor in my sight.' Now therefore, I pray thee, if I have found favor in Thy sight, show me now thy ways, that I may know thee, and find favor in thy sight. Consider too that this nation is thy people." And God said, "My presence will go with you, and I will give you rest." And Moses said to God, "If thy presence will not go with me, do not carry us up from here. For how shall it be known that I have found favor in thy sight, I and thy people? Is it not in thy going with us, so that we are distinct, I and thy people, from all other people that are upon the face of the earth."

And God said to Moses, "This very thing that you have spoken I will do; for you have found favor in my sight, and I know you by name." Moses said, "I pray thee, show me thy glory," and God said, "I will make all my goodness pass before you, and will proclaim before you my name, 'Yahweh': and I will be gracious to whom I will be gracious, and will show mercy on whom I will show mercy."

RSV, adapted

Biblical Interpretation

Chapter 33 of Exodus explores many different themes, all of which involve Moses who speaks with God on behalf of Israel. The image of Moses is one of a strong and courageous person who works actively to secure God's care and forgiveness for the people. Moses assumes the role of "faithful advocate" in various stories in the book of Exodus, but no where more strongly than in Exodus 33:12-19.

Prior to the episode in these verses, the people of Israel had disobeyed God's instructions by building the golden calf, a flagrant act of defiance toward God. Consequently, God had decided not to accompany these chosen people on their journey any longer. At this point, God's servant Moses becomes an outspoken advocate for the people of Israel. Moses refuses to accept God's decision. In one sense, he begins a verbal wrestling match with God. He starts by saying, "See, thou sayest to me, 'bring up this people;' but thou hast not let me know whom thou wilt send with me." Some scholars note that the beginning of those sentences has the flavor of someone saying, "now look here!" This tone of familiarity seems consistent with the profound tone of friendship that undergirds God's relationship with Moses. In a sense, God was accustomed to speaking with Moses as one speaks to a friend (See Numbers 12:7-8, for example). This respectful friendship enabled Moses to blurt out "now look here" when he believed that God's decision was not the right one for Israel. Moses simply could not believe that God would forsake them by refusing to accompany them further. Like a friend in a heated disagreement, Moses wanted two things: 1) to understand God's purpose for the decision, and 2) to convince God to reverse the decision. Moses' words, therefore, sought both clarification and intercession on behalf of the people who had broken the covenant.

In verse 17 God indeed reverses the decision saying "this very thing that you have spoken I will do," and Moses' faithfulness and advocacy find satisfaction. Moses is pleased and asks God to "Show me thy glory," a new request which God grants by letting "all my goodness pass before you." God's willingness to do this is a vivid demonstration that God's anger is gone and that Israel's sins are forgiven. From then on there would be no place that the chosen people could go without God's presence! This portrayal of God shows a character that is as free with mercy as with judgment. The clarity of that fullness of character comes as a result of Moses' willingness to argue with God on behalf of a sinful people. Moses was God's faithful mediator.

JYS

Literary Interpretation

Ask—God Answers

Be a teacher
Be a nurse
Be a housewife, they said,
And I obeyed.

Be a lady
Be a child
Be a doormat, they demanded,
And I let them walk on me.

O God, can I be only
A teacher
A nurse
A housewife?

O God, must I always be
A lady
A child
A doormat?

O God, let me sometimes
Be a principal
Be a doctor
Be a full partner.

O God, I want to
Be a woman
Be a grownup
Be a walker on doormats

O God, thank you!
When I ask, I receive
When I seek, I find
When I knock, you answer.

BJB

Personal Reflection

Being a Christian woman and a "faithful advocate" is often a difficult combination. Most of us have been shaped by parents and church school teachers to be quietly respectful of decisions made by others. Yet in the Exodus story (33:12-19), Moses intervened on behalf of the Israelites in an assertive, courageous, almost "gutsy" way. The Israelites had committed a gross act of disobedience by building and worshipping the golden calf; and now God was giving them the harsh consequences they might expect for such disobedience. Most of us believe that when God issues a judgment, we should accept it. In our own daily lives we often acquiese to decisions made by authority figures, whether or not we agree with the decisions. Part of growing up as a woman has meant to accept the decisions with quiet respect.

In a church board meeting which recently took place in a small rural congregation, the board members were discussing whether or not to begin providing nursery service during Sunday morning worship. Several new families had begun attending, and they seemed to need assistance with their babies and toddlers. Two long-time dedicated church women, both deacons and grandmothers, spoke out adamantly against the nursery. They said that when their children were little, they liked having the children with them in the pews, "where they belonged." If no one provided a nursery for them, why should one be provided now, especially for newcomers who had not yet proved their loyalty to the congregation?

A newly-elected church board member in her twenties was attending the meeting, the first board meeting of her tenure. She spoke with me after the meeting, poignantly sorry for the passive role she took. She reported that she knew how much a nursery would mean to the young parents and how much they yearned for the quiet enrichment of worship, a quietness which was not possible as they tried to keep their toddlers still. But she had not spoken out. She admitted that she was afraid to speak against the two older women who carried so much responsibility in the church. She was afraid to challenge their view. But as she talked about the meeting afterward, she regretted not having been God's faithful mediator on behalf of the young families.

Moses loved God as deeply as any human being could. But when God made what Moses thought to be a wrong choice, Moses spoke out. This biblical story reminds us that to be God's servants sometimes means to go against the socialization which has taught many of us that to be "good Christians" means to appear agreeable even in the face of wrong. Being God's faithful mediator means speaking out for what we know is right even if the issue is difficult and adversary formidable.

JYS

Biblical Character

Genesis 18:22ff

Abraham

Abraham is another biblical character who can be described as a "faithful advocate." When God told Abraham about the hideous accusations that had been charged against Sodom and Gomorrah (Genesis 18:22), Abraham inquired, "Are you really going to destroy the innocent with the guilty?" Abraham immediately followed up by negotiating "if there are fifty innocent people in the city, will you destroy the whole city? Won't you spare it in order to save the fifty?" God responded to the negotiations and agreed, "If I find fifty innocent people in Sodom, I will spare the whole city for their sake." Abraham quickly went on, "Please forgive my boldness . . . but perhaps there will be only forty-five innocent people . . . will you destroy the whole city because there are five too few?" God gave in a bit more and assured Abraham that the city would not be destroyed if forty-five innocent people were found. Then Abraham continued the same argument, saying, "Perhaps there will only be forty." Then thirty. Then twenty. Then ten. God said, "I will not destroy it if there are ten."

Like Moses in the Exodus story, Abraham was so close with God that he had the courage to enter into fierce and energetic negotiations with God. It is amazing to consider the audacity that Abraham must have had to bargain with God about the numbers of innocent people needed to save Sodom. But Abraham was persistent; and God was flexible.

Modern descriptions of biblical heroes like Moses and Abraham often focus on their almost godlike characters. We rarely conceive of these people as tough bargainers and hard negotiators. Yet when they felt that their people were being treated in ways that seemed unjust, they spoke out, even if it meant arguing directly with God. Other biblical figures have been similarly assertive as intercessors. Amos (chapter 7) and Jeremiah (chapter 14) are examples. These old testament personalities who drive hard bargains with God to secure justice for human beings provide a backdrop for Christ's later role as the true mediator between God and persons.

JYS

Historical Characters

Many women have been God's faithful mediators, most of them women whose names we have never heard. Rather than focus on one woman's role as a faithful advocate, and assertive worker for what is just and good, several nameless women will be lifted up. The readers will know some of these persons or persons like them!

_____ the Ohio woman who worked long, hard hours to establish a school and a playground area for migrant workers. She did this in the face of resistance from church members who were troubled by the dirt that the migrants would bring into the church fellowship hall. She said "no" to superficial stereotypes and the injustice that they bring, and she said a loud "YES" to kind, loving treatment for all of God's children.

_____ the pillar of the church who discovered she had cancer and who cooperated with physicians using traditional medical methods until she decided that they were too limited. From that point on, she did all in her power to enlist her mind, her friends, prayer, and her physical resources to fight the disease. Today she is still saying "no" to early death, and in her gentle, feisty way is saying "YES" to a longer life. Ironically, the power of her "yes" to life came from her saying "yes" also to death. To gain strength for her fight, she has enlisted the support of her family and her church friends. Her inspirational fight against the illness has so empowered her friends that what is heard now is a loud chorus of "Yes" on her behalf.

_____ the church woman whose life looked tranquil on the surface but who was criticized by her husband and who believed his insults until through the help of her close friends, she realized that she had to say "no" to that demeaning treatment. Her "no" was criticized by her church because some of the church members preferred the appearance of a happy marriage rather than public acknowledgement that things just weren't right. Her "no" meant pain and hurt for her and her family; but her loud "YES" was to a life of healthy, loving, Christian relationships.

These women, nameless, or recognized, are living examples of the commitment inside Moses that led him to argue with what seemed inevitable. These women argued on their own behalf and on behalf of others of God's precious children. For them we give thanks.

JYS

Worship Resource

Litany

Leader: For outspoken leaders like Moses and Abraham—
People: We thank you, God.
Leader: For persons who have the courage and the trust to challenge dcisions that seem immovable—
People: We thank you, God.
Leader: For feisty ones among us who say "No!" to cancer, "No!" to injustice, and "No!" to corporate insensitivity—
All: We thank you, God.
People: But in our thanks we confess that we have often been critical of these same courageous persons whom we praise. We have condemned their brashness and called them abrasive.
Leader: Forgive us, God.
People: Help us to understand that deep faith carries with it the responsibility to speak out for what is good and to question, at times, what seems certain. Help us to understand that you welcome our questions.
Leader: Be with us now and always, in the times that we accept your will quietly and the times when we cry out "No!"
All: Thank you, God, for your openness and for your promise that there is no where we can go where you are not.
Leader: No where we can go where you are not.
All: Amen.

JYS

Prayer

God, you are a loving and caring parent who watches over us every moment of our lives. We praise your reliability. We yearn for a world like the vision we have of your family, a family where all are secure in thc knowledge that they can go no where without you. We open ourselves to receive more clearly your will for us.

93

We thank you for the shower of blessings which you give us—
Our homes, families, health, choices,
wildflowers, ball games, physicians,
laughter, friends, the wind, our voices.
Help us to feel your flexibility and generosity even more than we do now.

Forgive us our many shortcomings—
our lack of gratitude,
our lack of courage,
our envy,
our silence in the face of injustice.

Forgive us, too, our defenses against your grace. Help us to believe that your grace for us is real—
even when we are indecisive
even when we are not perfect housekeepers
even when we are full of questions.

Enable us to realize that your forgiveness is already here and that we simply need to be open to receive it.

Guide us toward more courageous living. When we feel pulled toward the temptation of living in surface things, in transient beauty, and in weakhearted commitment, show us again your beautiful vision. Open our eyes.

We ask this help, forgiveness, and guidance from you today, our God. And we praise you and thank you each moment for your unending love. Amen.

JYS

Gleaning in Boaz's Field

Ruth 2:8-13

Then Boaz said to Ruth, "Now, listen, my daughter, do not go to glean in another field or leave this one, but keep close to my maidens. Let your eyes be upon the field which they are reaping, and go after them. Have I not charged the young men not to molest you? And when you are thirsty, go to the vessels and drink what the young men have drawn." Then she fell on her face, bowing to the ground, and said to him, "Why have I found favor in your eyes, that you should take notice of me, when I am a foreigner?" But Boaz answered her, "All that you have done for your mother-in-law since the death of your husband has been fully told me, and how you left your father and mother and your native land and came to people that you did not know before. God recompense you for what you have done, and a full reward be given you by Jahweh, the God of Israel, under whose wings you have come to take refuge!" Then she said, "You are most gracious to me sire, for you have comforted me and spoken kindly to your maidservant, though I am not one of your maidservants."

RSV, adapted

Biblical Interpretation

Ruth 2:8-13 records a conversation between Boaz and Ruth. The larger context is important! Ruth has made covenant with her mother-in-law, Naomi. She has stated in very certain terms that Naomi's destiny is her own destiny. "I will go WITH you!"

The story then moves rapidly. Ruth, in order to provide for herself and for Naomi, ventures out to the fields to glean grain (which is always left for widows, strangers, the poor, the oppressed). Boaz notices Ruth's coming day after day.

Now the conversation happens. Boaz gives Ruth instructions—instructions which are for Ruth's protection. "Stay in *this* field. Stay among *these* women. Gather where they gather. No one will harm you. And when you need a drink, help yourself."

Ruth expresses her respect for this person who cares about her welfare. Then she turns to Boaz with a question: "Why are you doing these things for me? I am a stranger. You are not obligated to offer me protection or nourishment. Why?"

Boaz answers Ruth's questions with a recital of RUTH's own deeds. "I know about your promises to Naomi. I know how much you have risked. You have given up everything to be with Naomi!" Then Boaz proclaims—"May Yahweh be to you as you have been with Naomi."

In her own caring way, Ruth responds to Boaz: "You also are kind and generous, for you have spoken to me in affirming ways. You did not have to. I am not a member of your family."

The conversation is a wonderful portrayal of GIFTS AND GRACE. Boaz is giving freely to Ruth who has already given so freely and generously to Naomi.

And so we can begin to SEE who Yahweh is . . . this One-who-is-with-us.

EHMcG

Literary Interpretation

The image of Yahweh
      as faithful friend
      as the stranger who wanders with me
   is crucial
      for my faith
      for my ability to trust.

As I experience
    with my friend
        immense loyalty
        mutual sharing
        intimate connectedness
        freeing laughter
  so I know Ruth
  so I know Yahweh
      the One who promises covenant love
      the One who is willing to be wounded
      the One who laughs with each new birth
I long to call
    all women to "Naomi and Ruth" relationships
I long for
    women to be that foolish
        that wise
        that loyal
        that strong
I long for
    my sisters to turn worlds upside-down
        to risk the unknown
        to get on with the journey
        to dare to promise
                as much as Ruth dared!

                        EHMcG

Personal Reflection

This passage from the Book of Ruth is most often interpreted as showing how God is seen in the person of Boaz—as a generous God who is gracious to the foreigner/stranger who is represented by the person of Ruth.

In such a patriarchal society, of course, the man Boaz is portrayed as the one who can give and protect and nourish.

Yet, if you will allow yourself to imagine in new ways, you can begin to SEE that Boaz is only beginning to act like Ruth has already acted.

Ruth has already offered her whole self—all her allegiance, her life, everything to Naomi. What more gracious act can you imagine?

Not only is Ruth gracious to Naomi; not only does her graciousness permit and encourage Boaz to act in such gracious ways, but the conversation in Ruth 2:8-13 shows us more of the qualities which show us who Ruth is.

Ruth is strong and a hard worker. She is loyal in doing the tasks she chooses for herself.

Ruth is willing to assert herself, to challenge Boaz about why he is doing these kind things for her.

Ruth is kind and gentle as she responds to Boaz's praise for who she is. She accepts the compliments graciously and lets Boaz know how she has experienced him.

Ruth is honest and straightforward as she relates to both men and women.

Perhaps the most radical possibility in this story is that ideas about who Yahweh is are turned upside-down. One would start out thinking Boaz is the Giver of Gifts, the model for Yahweh. YET as this conversation records, it is Ruth who is the model for Yahweh. Ruth has acted as Yahweh would! Ruth has been the One who risks everything to go with another. Ruth models the One who gives refuge—not in a stationary way, but in this revolutionary, on-the-move way!

Ruth is the Giver of Gifts!

EHMcG

Biblical Character

based on Luke 18:1-8

The Widow and the Unjust Judge

Ruth is so assertive, so trusting, so much the model of faithful friend. Are there any other women like her in the Biblical materials?

Look with me at Luke 18:1-8. This woman, like so many, is nameless and almost faceless. Yet, look! This woman, this widow, like Ruth, is assertive and forceful.

This woman demands justice from an unjust judge. DEMANDS! Over and over. She is persistent as Ruth has been persistent with Naomi.

Here again, if one is willing to risk imagination and seeing another way, one begins to realize that this story in Luke is not about the judge but about the character of this woman.

The unjust judge finally vindicates the woman. Then Jesus raises several questions: "Will not God be even more JUST than such an unjust judge as this? I wonder whether there is faith anywhere among you people! Are there others like this woman who have the courage, the conviction, the trust to DEMAND that justice be done?"

Will you SEE that Ruth knew who she was and what she wanted? She made choices and then worked to bring life into those choices.

This nameless woman whose story is recorded in Luke 18 is another "Ruth" who knew WHO she was and that justice could be done! She, like Ruth, made choices and commitments and moved actively and in trust toward creating that new reality.

EHMcG

99

Historical Character

I Have a Dream

A historical figure? This was a dilemma when I was asked to write about Ruth. We women, so many of us anyway, have no historical characters—we have had no mentors. But some of us do have good friends—deep, caring, risking friends. Yes, I have a friend who is like Ruth to me:

I have a dream of one whose story is
    of "Ruth"
    of persistent stranger
    of assertive widow.
I have a dream of one who knows her own self
    to be like Yahweh's self.
She is wise
    a kind of wisdom which is not of facts and data.
    Wisdom which is a knowing of her self
    a knowing of her own struggles and of her own gifts.
She is careful with words,
    like Ruth, choosing each word so that it expresses
      the depth of her love and commitment
    like the widow, mulling over and demanding at the right
      moments the RIGHT to speak.
She is at home with silence
    living with gentleness with all creation
    moving through each day simply offering the hospitality
      of safe space for every child who comes.
She is promise-maker
    risking a life of loyalty
    unafraid to journey on into the world of not-knowing
    open to trusting her own feelings and feeling with others.
She is "Ruth"
    full of grace
    free giver.

EHMcG

Worship Resource

Our Lament (together)

    We women would cry out
      in our shared and individual pain—
        Where is there ONE who will hear us?
        Where is there ONE who knows us?
        Where is there One who will go with us?

SHARING   (Individuals or all in the group share their deepest
            pain or hurt—be specific)

  ALL (together)
    Grace Giver!
        Come to us!
        Answer us!
        Nourish us!
        Do justice to us!

SPEECH OF SALVATION (from the mouth of a "Ruth")
    I will never leave you.
    Wherever you go, I will go with you!
    Wherever you live, I will live also.
    Your sisters are my sisters!
    Whenever you are in pain, I am in pain.
    Your life is my life.
    Your suffering is my suffering.
    We are bound together by our promises.
    Together justice will be done!

EHMcG

101

Prayer

Suffering Partner
Grace Giver
One who goes with us—
    We trust You.
    We have learned about You
        from the "Naomis in our lives—
            the mothers-in-law who loved us
                as though we were their own children.
    We remember!
      The journey is long and hard.
      We get tired of living in a foreign land.
      We are filled with anger and bitterness
          for all the losses.
            we experience.
      Travel with us!
      Give us peaceful rest.
      Let us rage
         and weep.
      Free us to be honest
         and to claim what we want and need.
      Make us brave enough
            to promise another woman solidarity.
And we will remember!
    We will go with You—
    We will offer grace to others.
    And we will continue
        to risk the pain
        the suffering
           that freedom might come!

EHMcG

Can A Woman Forget
Her Sucking Child

Isaiah 49:14-15

But Zion said, "God has forsaken me,
my God has forgotten me."
"Can a woman forget her sucking child,
that she should have no compassion
on the child of her womb?
"Even these may forget,
yet I will not forget you."

RSV adapted

Biblical Interpretation

The setting is Babylon during the late Jewish captivity. As the exiles gather for worship on the Sabbath the prophet Isaiah comes among them with words of comfort, hope and instruction. These people living out the decline of the Babylonian Empire feel undercurrents and movement of change, much as we do today, and they reflect it.

There is a transition and sudden shift in mood in this passage of scripture and the previous verses. The cry of verses 14 and 15 comes in sharp contrast to the joy and jubilation that had gone before. One moment the people feel confident: "All is well!" The next moment they feel terror: "All will surely perish!" How like small children they were, one moment smiling, the next fearful, crying and needing assurance.

The prophet tells them that indeed God *is* like a sensitive mother, who when she hears the cry of her nursing baby hurries to care for it. God is like a mother who simply cannot help but remember her frightened child and go to soothe her. Isaiah says, "God is your mother. God cannot keep from heeding your cry. Furthermore, because God's mothering nature is so much greater than a human woman's mothering nature, God's capacity to remember and have compassion is infinitely greater than a human mother's."

A mother does not usually turn aside from her needy child. Instead she gathers a hungry baby in her arms, calms and feeds it—often from her own breast. The child responds with eagerness and contentment. God's grace can be likened to this gift of food, love and compassion which a mother gives to her baby. The gift is freely given. It is unearned, but it is more than a mere gift, for it radiates the generosity and love of the giver. It also generates a response in the receiver. Just as the mother and child give and respond to each other, so do God and the Israelites in exile give and respond.

PJS

Literary Interpretation

How oft like little children
Who in a crowded mall
Turn from their loving mothers
And fail to hear their call
We turn from our creator
And think that we are lost
But God is searching for us
Regardless of the cost.

"Why have you left us Mother?"
Children cry in fright and pain,
And then they turn around once more
And they are found again.
We too can turn as children
In pain and fear and strife
To find that we are found again
By the source of love and life.

BJB

Personal Reflection

Optimistic, hopeful, cheerful and caring are words that are often used to describe me. I have been blessed with wonderful parents, a husband and children who love me and many, many friends. I am usually in excellent health. I have a job that is meaningful and satisfying. How could I ever become depressed? But it happened.

Life became dull, flat and hopeless. I had trouble sleeping, food lost its flavor. Some days I wondered if I could put one foot in front of the other to walk. The simplest job became difficult. I was always tired. I remember thinking, "How can I continue living, if this is all that life holds?"

I knew intellectually that my family still loved me. I tried meditation, prayer, even exercise. Nothing seemed to help. It was so hard to admit defeat. I had always been able to rely on my own strength.

Finally, when life seemed totally worthless, I asked for help from another. I could not do it alone. A psychologist became the image of God's grace for me. A person who could help me. What a joy! Life again became hopeful and optimistic. I could feel loved and cared for again. I was not abandoned. God's grace is a gift, always available, but I need help to be able to claim it.

LDI

Biblical Character

Luke 1:26ff

Mary and Elizabeth

The story of Mary and Elizabeth has elements of the interchange between Zion and God found in Isaiah 40:14-15. Certainly the young betrothed woman, Mary, had moments of hesitancy, doubt and disbelief as she sat alone.

Is it really true? Did I see and hear an angel? Will I soon have a baby? I have no husband, what shall I tell Joseph? If all this is really true, what should I do now?"

Then she remembers the angel had said Elizabeth is in her sixth month. She will visit Elizabeth. Hastily, she collects necessities for the journey and departs. As she nears her destination, again come the fears and questions: "Will Elizabeth welcome me? What if she doesn't believe my story of the angel? Oh God, what will become of me?" Even as she doubts, Mary arrives at the home of Elizabeth and Zachariah. She now knows the message she had heard is true—for Elizabeth, obviously pregnant, embraces her, hears her story and welcomes her.

Mary may have cried, as did Zion, "God has forsaken me, my God has forgotten me." Yet here in this home she experiences grace freely given through the persons of Elizabeth and—probably—Zachariah. Elizabeth could easily have been keenly jealous of this younger woman who claimed to be the future mother of the "Child of the Most High," but she was not. Even as Elizabeth saw Mary she bubbled over with the Holy Spirit and cried out, "Blessed are you among women." There is nothing to indicate that Elizabeth was anything but supportive of Mary, or that Mary in turn was not helpful during the remaining months of Elizabeth's pregnancy. Here are love and grace.

How often have I, like Mary may have, cried, "Where are you, God?" And just as I began to feel that awful loneliness, God in the person of another has come, put an arm around me and said, "I've been wondering about you. Tell me about it. What can I do to help?" Grace comes as a gift, undeserved. Surely if we human beings remember and care, how much greater and more secure must be the Grace of our God.

PJS

Historical Character

Carolyn Koons

Could anyone feel less loved? A nine-year-old boy in a Mexican prison accused of murder by parents who abandoned him. Could anyone care for this child? A child forced to live by his wits, beaten by bigger boys and the prison guards?

Carolyn Koons, a teacher at Azusa Pacific University, who takes college youth to Mexico each Easter season, was drawn to this boy. As the students played and sang at the prison, he became transformed. His eyes danced. His face lit up, and Carolyn, with other leaders, knew they must work for the release of this boy.

After many months, and years, of struggle to overcome the "roadblocks" and red tape of the Mexican justice system, Carolyn ultimately was able to secure the release of the young man, now called Tony. Bringing him to the United States, learning to be a mother, adopting him as a son, all point to the grace of God working through a person. When hope seemed gone for Tony to be released, when life together seemed threatened, God's love triumphed.

LDI

Worship Resource

Faith, Hope and Love (A Hymn)

Tune: A Swiss Yodeling Melody:
"Yodel with Me" by Josef Marais, 1952
Fideree Music Corporation
Sing Through the Seasons, p. 42.

For faith which can
    banish the terror of night
And bridge the cold chasm
    to put fear to flight,
For tender compassion
    which heals and redeems
I lift up my voice and
    thank God for new dreams.

Chorus:

God is my refuge
    and God is my strength.
God is my freedom and joy.

For hope which transcends
    the dark night of despair
And lifts up the spirit to
    transforming prayer,
For beauty which envelopes
    like the scent of a flower,
I lift up my voice
    and thank God for this hour.

For love which is deeper
    than passion or lust,
Which cares and which champions
                    the lost and the just;

For love which connects
to God's infinite law
I open my heart to its
limitless call.

LW

Prayer

O God, even Jesus cried out "Why have you forsaken me, O God!"
We all feel at times forsaken, left out, dry of inspiration, dreadfully
dreadfully alone.

When those times come O God, let us remember how touching,
how loving, a mother and her nursing child appear. How sweet
that communion, how satisfying and joyful.

Then let us recall that even when human love as tender as this
fails, you are still present for us. You will not leave us or forget us.
Help us to see past the feelings of lostness to the warmth of your
love.

Amen.

BJB

Anointed with Tears

Luke 7:36-50

One of the Pharisees asked Jesus to eat with him, and Jesus went into the Pharisee's house and took a place at the table. And behold, a woman of the city, who was a sinner, when she learned that Jesus was at table in the Pharisee's house, brought an alabaster flask of ointment, and standing behind Jesus at Jesus' feet, weeping, she began to wet those feet with her tears and wiped them with the hair of her head and kissed them and anointed them with the ointment. Now when the Pharisee who had invited Jesus saw it, he said to himself, "If this Jesus were a prophet, Jesus would have known who and what sort of woman this is who is doing the touching and anointing, for she is a sinner." And Jesus, answering said to him, "Simon, I have something to say to you." And Simon answered, "What is it, Teacher." "A certain creditor had two debtors; one owed five hundred denarii, and the other fifty. When they could not pay, the creditor forgave them both. Now which of them will love the creditor more?" Simon answered. "The one, I suppose, to whom the creditor forgave more." And Jesus said to him, "You have judged rightly." Then turning toward the woman Jesus said to Simon, "Do you see this woman? I entered your house, you gave me no water for my feet, but she has wet my feet with her tears and wiped them with her hair. You gave me no kiss, but from the time I came in she has not ceased to kiss my feet. You did not anoint my head with oil, but she has anointed my feet with ointment. Therefore I tell you, her sins which are many are forgiven, for she loved much; but one who is forgiven little, loves little." And Jesus said to her, "Your sins are forgiven." Then those who were at table with Jesus began to say among themselves, "Who is this, who even forgives sins?" And Jesus said to the woman, "Your faith has saved you; go in peace.

RSV adapted

Biblical Interpretation

There are stories of a woman anointing Jesus in each of the Gospels. This account in Luke focuses on Jesus' forgiving a sinful woman and the woman being very thankful.

Jesus was at the home of Simon the Pharisee. The New Testament Pharisees were people who stressed laws and rules and rigorously followed these legalisms. At first the Pharisee thought Jesus might be ignorant of the city woman's background, but he thought a prophet should automatically know what kind of woman she was. Thus, when the Pharisee realized that Jesus approved of this woman's anointing, the Pharisee was appalled. A great prophet, if Jesus were a prophet, should not have associated with such unworthy, sinful people.

The woman arrived with great humility and thankfulness. She proceeded to stand behind Jesus, anointing Jesus' feet while she was crying. She then wiped the oil and tears away with her hair. Standing behind Jesus, who lay at the table in the then current fashion, and anointing Jesus' feet were even more humble ways of anointing than the Matthew 26 or Mark 14 passages where Jesus' head was anointed. These other two passages do not mention whether the anointing occurred from behind.

Jesus went on to use a parable to explain the situation to Simon and the other Pharisees present. The story was that two people owed differing amounts to a creditor and the creditor forgave both of the debts. Jesus compared this to the situation at Simon's house. This woman who had many sins and was forgiven, loved God more than the Pharisees who rigorously tried to keep all the laws and sinned little (in their own eyes). Of course the Pharisees were furious as they felt that they were better law keepers and thus loved God more. And Jesus, the great prophet, sat in the home of a Pharisee and told them that a sinful woman loved their God more and was more appreciative of God's love than they were.

The passage ends as Jesus sends the woman on her way. She probably bounced and glowed with joy and appreciation. The Pharisees were muttering to each other and wondering about this prophet Jesus.

BW

Literary Interpretation

A Paraphrase of Psalm 106:1-6, 47-48

Praise our gracious God.
Praise our God who is good now and has and will always be good.
None of us can measure up to our Maker nor thank God enough for
all that has been done for us.

Yahweh, You look upon us with favor when we try to live according to Christ's example.
Remember us as we try and when You bestow grace upon earthly
people.
Let us be able to call ourselves Your children, that we may see
justice throughout the world and that we may love You enough
to want to witness to others.
We have all sinned. Help us to be thankful when You forgive the
sins in others, even sins that we feel are worse than our own.

Please save us from jealousy, pride, and lack of appreciation. May
You forever be our God, a very blessed God.
Amen and Amen.

BW

Personal Reflection

I find it easier to identify with the Pharisees in this story than the
woman from the city. I've been working long and hard to understand the life of Jesus Christ, and I appreciate and love God and the
grace God provides for us to continue the Christian journey.

Yet God also calls the "women and men of the city." Maybe this
group includes a thirty-year-old man I met while working at a
soup kitchen in Des Moines, Iowa. His life history was not a pleasant one. Then he raped an innocent nine-year-old girl.

When Jesus spoke the parable of forgiveness, did he mean that this man might be forgiven and be more thankful and love God more than I?

This is a challenge to me. Surely I, too, have sins to be forgiven and even greater love to develop for a gracious, although sometimes puzzling, God.

BW

Biblical Character

based on Luke 8:2, 24:10; Matthew 27:52-28:1;
Mark 15:40-16:9; John 19:25, 20:1,18

Mary Magdalene

Mary Magdalene was another Biblical character who had a changed life and followed Jesus. Some authors speculate that the "woman of the city" in Luke 7 may have been Mary Magdalene. Recent opinion does not support this.

What we know about Mary Magdalene is scattered through the gospels and is perhaps confused since there are several Marys. In Luke 8:2, Luke spoke of "some women who had been healed of evil and infirmities: Mary, called Magdalene, from whom seven demons had gone out . . ." Jesus had done this healing and forgiving of sins.

In John 12:3, Mary of Bethany, the sister of Martha, graciously anointed Jesus. It was a sign of gratitude, hospitality and love. Although the anointing was similar to that in Luke, Mary of Bethany cannot be equated with either Mary Magdalene or the "woman of the city."

The contact between Jesus and Mary Magdalene did not end with her healing, however. Mary was at both the crucifixion and burial of Jesus. Mary Magdalene was also the first person who saw Jesus after the resurrection. Imagine the emotions Mary felt when she saw a risen Jesus.

Mary Magdalene was only one of many people included in the Bible who made the switch from sinner to child of God. Mary's switch was from a woman containing seven demons to a close friend of Jesus. God provided grace then and provides grace now.

BW

Historical Characters

Anna Lee Hisey and Sally

Among the many people in the Church of the Brethren who outwardly reflect a joyous sense of grace is Anna Lee Hisey. Growing up in the Brethren territory of Bridgewater, Virginia, Anna Lee learned about faith and grace and living one's life for others. By the age of twenty-two, Anna Lee moved to Dundalk, Maryland for a Brethren Volunteer Service assignment. Here she could use her gifts to spread God's love.

Anna Lee began work with counseling and soon was helping to open the Family Crisis Center. This work provides services for abused women and children who are at a very low point in their lives. One such situation was with a woman we've renamed Sally.

Sally had been emotionally abused seven years by an alcoholic husband who isolated her from friends. Upon her arrival at the Shelter, Sally apologized for existing. She was insecure, had a low self esteem and was embarrassed with her situation. Personnel at the Center, including Anna Lee, helped with counseling and support as Sally began anew to find an apartment and regain custody of her children. Sally became close to Jesus Christ and gained power from this new relationship.

The ending is a happy one. Sally came back to the Center to say "thanks" by volunteering to help others in similar situations. She remains thankful to Christ despite her emotional, physical and family struggles. She also telephoned Anna Lee to say thank you for coming into her life when she was most needed. She feels much to be thankful for and remembers to express it.

As for Anna Lee, she, too, is touched by God working through the life of Sally and the lives of many other Sallys. After receiving a thank you from Sally, Anna Lee commented, "She made me realize how grateful I should be for the grace of God in my life caring for me." And it has been many years since Christ first began to work through Anna Lee's life.

At Simon's home, the woman overtly expressed her excitement at a changed life. This kind of excitement and change did not end at Simon the Pharisee's house. It continues now through Sally and Anna Lee and many more.

BW

Worship Resource

Unison Reading

We recognize that we sometimes act as Pharisees and sometimes act as the sinning woman of the city. We recognize that neither is how we are to live. We recognize that you, God, are our release from both ways of life.

Let us remember the grace that comes only from you. Mrs. W. J. Kennedy expressed it in the words, "O how wondrous the grace of our God, how sweet and how joyous the thought, that Christ ransomed our souls . . ."

Let us remember the grace that changes lives. Famous words from John Newton express this as, "Amazing grace . . . that saves a wretch like me . . ."

Let us remember the grace that continues with us day after day. Another songwriter, Julia Johnston, wrote, "Marvelous grace of our loving [God], grace that exceeds our sin and our guilt . . ."

We have been forgiven through God's grace. Let us remember this grace throughout our days.

BW

Prayer

Our God,
As I go through changes in life, help me realize that I:
    never escape from sin
    never escape from needing you
    never escape from your grace.
But this world is so much larger than I am. Help me to:
    help others search for encouragement
    help others search for love
    help others search for your grace.
Strengthen me to be your presence on earth. Let me:
    tell others of your grace
    show others your love
    speak to others some words of encouragement.
Help me to be more thankful for:
    your providing Jesus Christ
    my chance to be your witness in the world
      and in my community
    new insights even in old stories.
And let me remember Simon, the woman of the city, Sally, Anna
Lee, and Mary Magdalene and the way you have used each of these.
    Amen.

BW

Imperishable Jewels

I Peter 3:3-4

Let not your behavior be the outward adorning with braiding of hair, decoration of gold and wearing of fine clothing, but let it be the hidden person of the heart with the imperishable jewels of a gentle and quiet spirit, which in God's sight is very precious.

RSV adapted

Biblical Interpretation

Portions of I Peter have often been used to keep women in their place. The interpretation has been, "The man is the head of the house. Women dress with plainness. Don't wear jewelry."

Commentaries on I and II Peter speak of the social structure at the time of the early church. And Peter clearly writes from within that structure in which women were practically the property of their husbands.

But just because our times are different does not mean that Peter's advice has no value today. If we look beyond what seems to be a negative message about outward adornment in I Peter 3:3 and beyond our deeply ingrained feelings about how we have been preached at from this passage, we may be able to see the comfort—and beauty—that are available to us.

A related scripture can prevent us from being overly offended by Peter. Jesus frequently spoke about the importance of the inner self. "Woe to you, scribes and Pharisees, hypocrites! for you cleanse the outside of the cup and of the plate, but inside they are full of extortion and rapacity. You blind Pharisees! first cleanse the inside of the cup and of the plate that the outside may also be clean." (Matt. 23: 25-26 RSV)

Peter reinforces this notion. What counts is what is inside—within the hidden person of the heart. Having confidence in outward adornment may mean that we don't understand or accept the beauty that God has placed within us.

To accept God as creator is to believe that we were molded by a skilled craftsperson who does not create ugly objects. To accept God as sustainer is to believe that God makes available to us a quiet and gentle spirit—wholeness.

A quiet and gentle spirit is not passive or colorless. We see the manner in which Jesus combined strength and wholeness with a quiet and gentle spirit. The same spirit can be with us as we protest injustice, as we work tirelessly for world peace, as we deal with obstreperous children, as we experience crisis in our marriages, as we work under the pressures of our jobs.

That spirit is a jewel, and it makes us beautiful.

NP

Literary Interpretation

A Fable of Two Women

Two women dwelt side by side, each as lovely as the other, each acclaimed by the community for her beauty. One had her hair professionally set at least twice a week, traveled to Chicago, or Dallas or New York City to be sure she dressed in the latest fashion, had an account at Tiffany's to make certain she could adorn herself with the most beautiful jewels in the most stylish settings. She regularly attended workshops on how to apply makeup to highlight her "best features" and spent several weeks each year at a popular health and beauty spa so her face and figure were always at their best.

The other washed her hair in the shower and set it by running a comb through it on her way to a meeting of the community chest board, served as a high school counselor through the day and as a volunteer at the teen drop in center two nights a week. She could always be counted on to attend workshops on Christian Education, and music and worship, and try to use the ideas she learned about in the local church. She also spent several weeks each year as a camp counselor, or working at a refugee center.

Two women dwelt side by side, each lovely in her own way, one acclaimed by the community for the beauty of her body, the other, for the beauty of her soul.

BJB

Personal Reflection

Sometimes it's hard to be aware of our beauty, especially if we've been taught that attempts to be attractive are non-Christian. So instead of seeing imperishable jewels within ourselves, we see ordinary rocks.

We may think, "I'm ordinary. I'll appear ordinary." So our drab, unattractive exterior makes evident the plain rock that weighs down our hearts.

Or we decide to decorate the rock. We spend time, money, and energy on finding clothes and makeup that will make us appear more attractive, more competent, or more youthful.

Both attitudes can easily alienate us from those whose closeness we desire. The plain outward appearance may seem to reflect an inner drabness. Or people may see through a showy exterior and keep a distance.

Sometimes we meet someone whose beauty strikes us immediately. Perhaps she is dressed in clothing that she has obviously chosen with care. Or perhaps she is dressed simply and seems not to have put a lot of attention into her appearance. But in each case there is beauty within that seems to envelope the total person.

119

If we recognize the jewel of a quiet and gentle spirit that is within us, total beauty becomes available to us. We don't have to work at making our appearance show a beauty that we don't believe is really there. Nor do we consider our beauty sinful and try to hide it. By accepting the precious jewel that is within us, we are free to express our inward beauty in our outward appearance. Yet we know that because God's spirit is within us, we do not need to rely on outward adornment.

NP

Biblical Character

based on Luke 1:26-2:52

Mary, the Mother of Jesus

"My soul magnifies God," Mary said when she learned that she was pregnant with Jesus. "And my spirit rejoices in God my Saviour."

God now dwelt within her in a way that no other woman had or has since experienced. Can we not assume that the knowledge of God's presence within her made Mary's total being radiate the beauty of God's spirit?

We know nothing about Mary's physical appearance. She probably did not wear splendid robes or have her hair braided in the fancy fashion of the day. It's hard to imagine her looking her best during the biblical episodes we read. Surely after a tiresome ride to Nazareth on a donkey her clothing was disheveled and she looked exhausted. And when she missed twelve-year-old Jesus on that long trip home from the temple, she was probably dusty and had more than one hair out of place. It's inconceivable that she would have been concerned about how she was dressed or how she looked as she watched Jesus hanging from a cross.

Yet it would be difficult to locate a work of art that does not give Mary a beauty reflective of the artist's culture. Whether an Italian of the Middle Ages, a German of the eighteenth century, or a contemporary Japanese, Mary is depicted as a woman of beauty. Perhaps the artists express what we all sense—that to magnify God and rejoice in God as savior fills a person's spirit with beauty. And a beautiful spirit cannot be kept hidden within.

NP

Historical Character

Elizabeth Bayley Seton

Elizabeth Bayley Seton was the first American-born saint in the Roman Catholic Church. Her commitment to God gave birth to today's Catholic school system and to our country's Catholic orphanages and child-care centers.

In 1774, in New York City, Elizabeth Bayley was born into a well-known Episcopal family. Her father was a physician and the first professor of anatomy at Columbia Medical School.

Elizabeth was educated as a genteel young woman of that day and became a New York debutante. Yet her father did not shelter her from seeing how others lived. Frequently she accompanied him on his calls among the poor.

At the age of nineteen she married William Seton, also of an affluent family. But ten years after her marriage Elizabeth was a widow with five children and no money.

Under the tutelage of an Italian couple, she converted to Catholicism, a step that angered many of her friends. So she moved to Baltimore, a more religiously tolerant city, and with the help of Father DuBourg, established the first Catholic school in America.

Later, Elizabeth moved her own children and her school to property she had been given in Emmitsburg, Maryland. She also started a motherhouse for a religious community from which today's various branches of the Sisters of Charity trace their origins.

Elizabeth Seton spent her younger years wearing furs and jewels. She was known as a beautiful young woman. Later in her life she wore a wimple and was robed in black with no adornment other than her rosary beads. Yet people continued to be struck by her beauty.

NP

Worship Resource

Litany

One: Some people are able to recognize a precious stone among a cluster of rocks.

All: I confess, God, that I do not always recognize the jewel that you have placed within my heart.

One: An expert can cut the jewel with such precision that its facets brilliantly reflect the light.

All: Enable me to chip away the low self-esteem that sometimes makes me unattractive.

One: A patient craftsperson will polish the jewel and increase its luster.

All: Help me to increase my luster, not be depending on my outward appearance, but by grinding away at the self-centeredness that mars my beauty.

One: A careful jeweler places the gem firmly and securely within its setting.

All: May I accept the security and strength that you offer.

One: The confident owner will not flaunt the jewel so that all will admire it nor hide the jewel in a drawer so that no one will notice it.

All: May people see your beautiful spirit within me and glorify you.

NP

Prayer

God, thank you for creating me in your image, for giving me
your beautiful spirit.
I confess that often, when I look at the hidden person of my heart,
I see only ugliness.
Help me to grow in the understanding of my beauty
that I may grasp your spirit of quietness and gentleness;
that my outward appearance may be in harmony with the
loveliness in my heart.
Remove from my life self-centeredness
that I may bring beauty into the lives of those around me;
that I may recognize and affirm the beauty of others.
May those who see the beauty within me and those who discover
their own beauty through my caring spirit give you the praise.
Amen.

NP

To Heal the Broken

Of Pride and Prejudice

Numbers 12:9-15

And the anger of Yahweh was kindled against Miriam and Aaron and God departed; and when the cloud removed from over the tent, behold Miriam was leprous, as white as snow. And Aaron turned towards Miriam, and behold, she was leprous. And Aaron said to Moses, "Oh, my lord, do not punish us because we have done foolishly and have sinned. Let her not be as those dead, of whom the flesh is half consumed when they come out of their mothers' wombs." And Moses cried to Yahweh, "Heal her, O God, I beseech thee." But Yahweh said to Moses, "If her father or mother had but spit in her face, should she not be shamed seven days? Let her be shut up outside the camp seven days, and after that she may be brought in again." So Miriam was shut up outside the camp seven days; and the people did not set out on the march till Miriam was brought in again.

RSV adapted

Biblical Interpretation

And God came down in a pillar of cloud, and stood at the door of the tent, and called Aaron and Miriam . . . And God said, "Hear my words: . . . my servant Moses is entrusted with all my house. With him I speak mouth to mouth . . . and he beholds the form of God. Why then were you not afraid to speak against my servant Moses?" and behold, Miriam was leprous, as white as snow. Numbers 12:5-8, 10 (RSV adapted).

"Judge Not"—But Use Good Judgment

"Unclean! Unclean!" The horrifying words seared themselves into Miriam's consciousness. Did she have leprosy or didn't she? Why had she been so thoughtless and criticized Moses' wife? Would she be condemned to die?

What might have caused Miriam's leper-like disease? *The Interpreter's Bible* says that God never used leprosy as punishment for sin, suggesting that Miriam's infliction was probably not leprosy. One can almost see Miriam and Aaron trembling as they nervously inched toward the Tabernacle to receive their verdict from the angry Holy of Holies, who was enraged at their behavior in rejecting Moses' wife. Certainly the wrath of the Almighty caused great stain upon them at that time.

Modern medicine would likely classify Miriam's affliction as vitiligo or leucodermia, a "cutaneous disorder caused by severe emotional stress and characterized by the absence of pigment." Wholistic health experts might add that anxiety permeated Miriam's central nervous system and attacked the weakest link, causing psychosomatic illness. The lack of relationship with God, without whose help the Israelites could not survive, took its toll on Miriam. The real question, however, is not what disease Miriam had, but how she responded to the situation. Did she wallow in self-pity, feeling she deserved better treatment? Or did she rise above her mistakes?

Until Miriam knew, really knew, that she was free of leprosy, she undoubtedly lived a nightmarish existence. Certainly by the seventh day when the priest declared her whole, her heart sang a song of deliverance and she was all the wiser for her affliction.

Through her suffering Miriam learned responsibility for other human beings. Amending the truth of Jesus' statement to a later age—"Judge not, that you be not judged"—might be the added wisdom which all of us should glean from Miriam's experience: "Judge not" but use good judgment.

JJS

127

Literary Interpretation

And the anger of God was kindled against [Miriam and Aaron] . . . and behold, Miriam was leprous, as white as snow. And Moses cried to God, "Heal her, O God, I beseech thee." But God said to Moses . . . "Let her be shut up outside the camp seven days . . ." Numbers 12:9, 10, 13, 14 (RSV adapted).

I Miriam

How did it feel to be Miriam? Banished seven days from the children of Israel, Miriam could have felt remorse, impatience, anger, or any number of reactions. Just for a moment, let us suppose Miriam kept a diary . . . .

"Walls. How long have I stood outside these walls of my own making? Sometimes I don't understand God, and anger wells within me. Shouldn't Aaron have been punished, too? He didn't like Moses' choice of a wife any more than I did. Why isn't he sharing my shame in this barren wilderness?

"I know I'm not perfect, God, and I'm not always right. Yes, Aaron did intervene in my behalf, and when Moses saw the curse of whiteness upon my skin, he, whom I had condemned, cried out, "Heal her, O God.' But it was not to be.

"These are my people—that little band far off in the distance. My love for them must come first, before my own concerns. I could be angry, but I feel chastised instead.

"In spite of the shame my people place upon my breast, God is not nor ever was against us women. I know in my heart that I deliberately hurt my sister-in-law, Zipporah. Perhaps God's love for her is large enough to include both of us. Perhaps we are sisters and I must treat her so.

"Zipporah—I have sinned. My words were not from my heart: they were from ignorance of you—and of myself. And now I taste the bitterness of striking out against one of my own.

"As a daughter of the Mighty God, I should be nailing pieces of our relationship together rather than prying the structure of the human family apart.

"Zipporah, come to me. I am your sister now."

JJS

Personal Reflection

Let the nations be glad and sing for joy, for thou dost judge the
peoples with equity . . . Psalms 67:4 (RSV)

Miriam's Ministry: Prophet

In the process of studying the character of Miriam I find myself, as a woman, identifying with her. Had Hebrew society been prone to looking to women for leadership, would God have chosen Miriam instead of Moses or Aaron to fulfill the Divine Will for the children of Israel? How many times in history has God circumvented the supreme plan to choose a man to do a job simply because the human race was not open to God's calling of women?

How sad it is that God has been unable to use half the human race to further the work of heaven. I myself have felt the clash between society's and God's will for my personal life.

At the age of eleven, when my Aunt Helen entered Bethany Seminary, I also made a commitment to enter the Christian ministry. After being licensed to preach in Southern Pennsylvania at age 17, I entered college in 1962 to major in religion. After years of patiently waiting, my preparation for Christian service had finally begun.

Shortly after graduation I became engaged. Since my fiance was attending Bethany we naturally wondered how two ministers in the same family might get along.

I sought the opinion of others. One said, "Don't do it." Another added, "You will argue whose church it is." (Today I ask: *"Whose* church is it—ours or God's?") Yet another told me, "You cannot marry a church and a husband, too. It will never work." No one asked what I felt the will of God was for my life.

With great sorrow I dropped the license, and I have lived to regret the moment that decision was made. Within five years attitudes had changed and women were entering seminary with their husbands.

Yet God has been gracious to this frustrated preacher. Today, through McPherson College and the Christian education which it offers I am able to reach out and touch lives of young persons in a deeply meaningful way, and I am grateful to God for opening another avenue of ministry to me.

For me it may be too late. But for younger women everywhere, the church has an exciting future ahead as God opens doors to use the potential of both men *and* women, *all* of the human race.

JJS

Biblical Character

Miriam and Aaron spoke against Moses because of the Cushite woman whom he had married . . . and the anger of God was kindled against them." Numbers 12: 1, 9 (RSV adapted).

The God Who Expects

Many speak openly of times when God opened doors for them, but few talk freely of times when the doors have been closed. Perhaps the pain of such experience elicits feelings of failure or inadequacy. Yet when viewing our lives from God's perspective, such wilderness experiences may actually be doors opened.

Miriam had a way with words. Her sharp mind saved the life of the infant Moses. Later it opened the door of leadership, and she became a prophet to her people.

But power has a way of creating self conceit, and Miriam fell into the trap by criticizing Moses' wife. As often happens, her accusations revealed more about the complainer than they did of the one about whom she complained. As Ophelia said of the mutinous Hamlet, "Oh, what a noble mind is here o'erthrown." God surely expected more of Miriam.

As a caring parent sometimes isolates a child in a corner to give that child time to think, Miriam was sent into the wilderness.

Completely alone, with wild prowling animals by night and the scorching sun by day, seven days were undoubtedly enough to elicit compliance with the Almighty's will.

Probably the dark night of the soul for Miriam had both negative and positive effects. During low times she must have thought about her shortcomings as a sister and leader of her people. She might even have been driven to despair at the deprivation of body and soul which she experienced.

Yet even in times of their remorse and suffering, God comforts the mortal children of this earth. Certainly Miriam emerged chastised, but victorious from her encounter with God, who expected so much from her. By shutting one door God opened another and the impulsive Miriam became a thoughtful human being, considerably wiser, and consciously aware of others' feelings and pain.

Through her experience Miriam matured into the person God wanted her to be. Humility rather than arrogance is the trademark of God's servants. Through her humbling experience she could at last, at long last, fulfill her role as prophet for her God.

JJS

Historical Application

New Windows—New Worlds

Harvey and Addie Nininger, authors of *It Wasn't Always Meteorites*, became world-renowned in the science of meteorology. In their book they likened their years of education at McPherson College to that of a wanderer who chanced upon a musty old house in the forest. Prying boards from one window after another, the wanderer discovered a world of breathtaking beauty far surpassing anything ever experienced previously.

Taking the Nininger's metaphor one step further, one might surmise that faith is more than a skylight shedding light from above. Many believe that Christianity is a vertical relationship between oneself and God—the skylight effect—but fail to see the light of God which sheds itself horizontally over the earth, encompassing all races and every discipline of knowledge.

Faith is integrated into life. As James says, "Faith apart from works is dead." (James 2:26, RSV)

Miriam of the Old Testament assumed a religious relationship only between herself and God and not between herself and her brother, Moses and her sister-in-law Zipporah.

As the Quakers believe, a spark of the Divine is within us all, and we cannot look at our brothers and sisters, no matter what their race or ideology, without assuming that divine relationship. Isolation in the wilderness must certainly have helped Miriam to get a perspective on God's overall plan. It must surely have opened windows of knowledge to her and made her more accepting of the totality of God's creation including Moses' foreign wife, Zipporah.

Today, broadening our vision might mean admitting that Russians, those whom we know the least about and who pose the greatest threat—the Zipporahs of our age—are our sisters and brothers, too. They, also, possess the spark of the Divine. We need to perch above ourselves, alongside God, if only for a moment, to see life in its totality from God's perspective.

For God is a great God . . . In God's hands are the depths of the earth; . . . let the hills sing for joy together before God . . . God will judge the world with righteousness, and the peoples with equity." Psalms 95:3, 4; 98:7-9 (RSV adapted).

JJS

Worship Resource

But God said to Moses . . . "Let her be shut up outside the camp seven days . . . And the people did not set out on the march till Miriam was brought in again." Numbers 12: 14, 15 (RSV adapted).

All People Have Their Sins—A Conversation

One: I once heard our pastor say, "The ten commandments are the minimum which God expects of us, and the beatitudes are the maximum."

Other: That statement speaks of the higher calling of the Christian. Yet how many of us, when faced with realities of daily life, have difficulty with even the minimum expectations of God?

One: Miriam, sister of Aaron and Moses, was no exception. God quite obviously had looked with favor upon her, elevating her as a prophet to her people. Yet when Moses married a Cushite woman, Miriam saw only through her prejudice, rejecting Moses' actions openly and callously.

Other: The genius of the Bible is that its authors tell the stories of very human persons. Moses, beloved leader of the children of Israel, committed murder. Aaron, high priest and spokesperson for God through Moses, forged a golden calf for the Hebrews to worship. Even sister Miriam, who saved Moses' life when he was an infant, allowed a streak of prejudice to overrule common sense.

One: Yes, Miriam the prophet was human, too. Even she had difficulty following the basic ten. And God, who was displeased, sentenced her to the ostracism of her people for seven days. She had to straighten her priorities, to separate herself from the others, before she could return again.

Other: All people have their sins. And yet anyone who thinks God is stringent in the Old Testament should study Jesus' teachings in the New. Jesus went so far as to say that an evil thought in our hearts may find us guilty of breaking all of God's commandments.

One: Yet, forgiveness, too, is a part of the New Testament teachings. Jesus seems to require more in the beatitudes, but the love of Christ reaches deeper than God's judgment. We need to accept God's forgiveness of our human frailties, then press onward to become the persons Christ calls us to be.

JJS

Prayer

The King's daughter came down to the river to bathe . . . Suddenly she noticed the basket in the tall grass . . . The princess opened it and saw a baby boy . . . his sister asked her, "Shall I go and call a Hebrew woman to nurse the baby for you?" Exodus 2:5-7 (RSV).

Of Pride and Prejudice

O God,

Miriam was justly proud of her accomplishments when, as a child, she saved her brother Moses from the wrath of Egypt's pharaoh. As Miriam saw it, simply because she had the capacity to think clearly in that demanding situation, Moses was placed in the care of Pharoah's daughter who elevated this would-be Hebrew slave to a governor of the land.

And God, Miriam spent much of her life following Moses with the children of Israel. She undoubtedly harbored a sense of personal pride in her eminent sibling's accomplishments. And in her identification with Moses, Miriam very possibly claimed the occasional right to manipulate Moses' will.

As far as Miriam could see, O God, Moses had only one tragic flaw: he had married a foreign wife. Perhaps a Hebrew woman who could have shared in his ambitions might have been acceptable to Miriam, but not a foreigner—and a Cushite woman, at that. Her language was different, her culture was different, and some scholars say that the color of her skin was different, too. "How could this woman possibly identify with the importance of Moses' mission?" Miriam must have thought.

Sibling rivalry reared it ugly head. Miriam complained and Aaron, their brother, complained with her. Their accusations became so eloquent that the Bible says you became displeased and angry.

Had Moses been a young person caught in the throes of an unwise decision, perhaps guidance would have been in order. But he was mature, and Miriam had to learn to trust—her brother and you, O God, and even her own ability to "let go."

How many times, O God, do we, in dealing with relatives and friends, impose our values and expectations upon them? We need to look, as Miriam perhaps did after her illness and isolation, beyond our limited vision to the larger vision you have for all of us who in your infinite love are so much more accepting than we.

O God, when we judge others, chastise us, but we pray that you will not cast us out of your sight, that you will not separate us from your people!

Recall us to your clear mission for us—to serve you and your people—with pure hearts and open minds.

Amen.

JJS

To Heal the Broken

Isaiah 61:1-3

The Spirit of Yahweh God is upon me, because Yahweh has anointed me to bring good tidings to the poor and afflicted; God has sent me to bind up the brokenhearted, to proclaim liberty to the captives, and the opening of the prison to those who are bound in body or in spirit; to proclaim the year of Yahweh's favor, and the day of vengeance of our God; to comfort all who mourn; to grant to those who mourn in Zion—to give them a garland instead of ashes, the oil of gladness instead of mourning, the mantle of praise instead of a faint spirit; that they may be called oaks of righteousness, the planting of Yahweh, that God may be glorified.

RSV paraphrased

Biblical Interpretation

This scripture is one of the most quoted Biblical passages relating to social justice. When it is quoted the reference may be to the words of the prophet Isaiah or to Jesus and the choice of this passage to signal the tone of Christ's ministry (Luke 4). Both of them felt these words spoke to the suffering of the people.

Good news to the poor. Isaiah saw all about, the suffering of the poor, their hunger, their homelessness, their oppression as workers, their bondage through violent taskmasters, robbed of land and dignity. Surely not to be poor any more, nor hungry, nor homeless would be the best news they could receive.

Bind up the brokenhearted. Who is a brokenhearted person? I believe that heart refers here to spirit, persons whose spirit is broken. That takes us to those poor again, whose spirits are broken by complete hopelessness, by seeing their children born into the same enslaving system, by feelings of helplessness and fear and absolutely no recourse. A broken spirit is not easily repaired.

Liberty to the captives. A system as degraded as the one Isaiah spoke to holds many people captive. Those whose bodies are actually in chains, in prisons. It enslaves those who rule in fear and use increasingly harsh measures to ensure their place of power. It enslaves the families of prisoners, of jailkeepers, of the rich and the military. Isaiah calls for liberty to the captives, all captives, a system where all people are freed from the many captivities that strangle and kill.

Comfort all who mourn. Mourning is an outward sign of deep inward pain, a pain that comes from personal loss of loved ones, but also from loss of land, job, of hope and dignity. The weeping of a nation was not lost on Isaiah.

To proclaim the year of God's favor. Isaiah's confidence in God is unshaken. God has offered the people a choice. Change their ways—and healing can take place.

RR

Literary Interpretation

In *Killers of the Dream*, Lillian Smith writes of the awakening of southern women to the evils of segregation and the sin of lynching:

And then it happened. The lady insurrectionists gathered together in one of our southern cities. They primly called themselves church women but churches were forgotten by everybody when they spoke their revolutionary words . . .

It may seem incredible, but the custom of lynching had rarely been questioned by the white group. The church women's action gave a genuine shock. This was a new thing in Dixie . . .

Of course the demagogues would have loved to call them "Communists" or "bolsheviks," but how could they? The women were too prim and neat and sweet and ladylike and churchly in their activities, and too many of them were the wives of the most powerful men in town. Indeed, the ladies themselves hated the word "radical" and were quick to turn against anyone who dared go further than they in this housecleaning of Dixie. Few of them had disciplined intellects or giant imaginations and probably no one of them grasped the full implications of this sex-race-religion-economics tangle, but they had warm hearts and powerful energy and nice technic for bargaining, and many an old cagey politician, and a young one or two, have been outwitted by their soft bending words . . .

They worked with great bravery but so unobtrusively that even today many southerners know little about them. But they aroused the conscience of the South and the whole country about lynching; they tore a big piece of this evil out of southern tradition, leaving a hole which no sane man in Dixie now dares stuff up with public defenses . . .

But they were not yet done. They had a few more spots to rub out. One had to do with their own souls. They believed that the Lord's [sic] Supper is a holy sacrament which Christians cannot take without sacrilege unless they will also break bread with fellow men [sic] of other color. Believing, they put on their best bib and tucker and gathered in small groups to eat with colored women, deliberately breaking a taboo that had collected many deep fears around it.

Reprinted from KILLERS OF THE DREAM
by Lillian Smith, by permission of
W. W. Norton & Company, Inc.
Copyright 1949, (c) 1961 by Lillian Smith

Personal Reflection

What caused Isaiah to be so outspoken concerning the evils he saw around him? He was a well-educated person, a courtier and an aristocrat. He was married and had a young son. It was time for a young man to settle down, become a part of the community, be responsible.

Isaiah chose another way. His response to God's call "Whom shall I send?" echoes through the centuries. "Here am I, send me." The responsibility was a heavy one. It is not easy, and seldom pleasant, to call attention to injustice. We're too likely to step on someone's toes, or pocketbook, or long-held prejudices. We're apt to be called names, to be charged with ulterior motives, or worse, to be ignored.

As I write this, a political campaign is in full swing in our country. And around the world, the brokenness that Isaiah decried exists in untold places, in the Philippines, Central and South America, Central and South Africa, Indonesia, South Korea, Kampuchea and in our own country. I long for a prophetic voice that would dare point out the self-interest, the economic advantage, the pride and dangerous patriotism that prevent healing where it is so needed.

Some few dare to make such a witness and are dismissed as onesided, as radicals or even as communists. Their message is discounted and their voices often stilled. Is truth so condemning?

Isaiah had the courage to call evil and sin by their rightful names, to place the responsibilty appropriately, to address those responsible and call them to accountability, to ultimately bring healing to brokenness.

Can I learn from Isaiah how to witness to my own deeply held convictions? I hope so. I believe valuable lessons can be learned from many sources, from those who suffer, from studying the motivation of the oppressors, from prophetic teachings and from searching for God's will in each situation. Isaiah also offers some solutions for healing. Sometimes solutions take as much courage as the denouncements and are subject to the same criticism, but they lead the way to healing.

RR

Biblical Character

based on Acts 18:1-3, 18-19, 24-28)

Priscilla

There's not a lot said about Priscilla, but she's very present in the early history of the Christian church. One writer, Harnack, has even suggested her as a possible author for the Epistle to the Hebrews! Sometimes she's known as Prisca. There's something about that I like. Not many Biblical personalities had nicknames, though there are unlimited possibilities. I think there must have been something special about her that encouraged this familiarity.

Prisca and her husband were tentmakers with whom Paul, also a tentmaker, often stayed. Can't you imagine these three working together, exchanging ideas, challenging and questioning each other and strengthening each other's faith? Such experiences must have built a recognition of truth and a sense of urgency that truth be proclaimed.

So a new preacher, Apollos, comes to town. A very charismatic personality, well trained in philosophy and the scriptures. Prisca and her husband heard him speak, but something was lacking. The only clue the scripture gives is that Apollos had "only the baptism of John."

In the light of the Isaiah text, I am tempted to draw some conclusions. That John's "baptism" or message was one of personal salvation only. Jesus enlarged that message to one of salvation *and* social responsibility. But Prisca's action is notable.

She and her husband went directly to Apollos, took him home and over a cup of coffee and some honey cake, they "expounded to him the way of God more perfectly." What daring—but it worked!

Here is another example of a way to witness to what we believe is truth. Sharing ideas with church leaders with whom we differ in understanding and in the interpretation of scripture is probably one of the most difficult tasks we could take on, threatening everyone involved. Theirs is a success story; ours might well turn out differently.

But Prisca dared. Can we do less?

RR

Historical Character

Lillian Smith

Lillian Smith grew up in the South in the early 1900s. She understood its traditions, social structure, taboos and violence and became one of the strongest voices in this century in behalf of racial equality and social justice.

I present her here as a courageous woman who used her talent to work at the brokenness she saw around her. Her most notable work was *Strange Fruit*, published in 1944, a controversial book that helped break the barrier of silence on racial matters.

Some of the controversy over the novel stemmed from the fact that a Southern woman was willing to oppose racial segregation by writing an exposé of segregation's degrading and inhumane aspects in the form of a novel.

Lillian Smith was deeply affected by her early life in a rigid, religion-centered home environment in a segregated community. She grew up knowing intimately the hurts and lasting wounds of brokenness and an overwhelming desire to remove all barriers between people of whatever kind.

I may have a more personal reason for being drawn to Lillian Smith. From 1953 till her death in 1966, she was incapacitated from time to time by recurrent cancer. She battled courageously on this front also and developed a concern for persons with physical handicaps and the barriers that separate them from others. [Editor's note: Ruby Rhoades lost her battle with cancer before this one of her many contributions to healing the broken could be published.]

Lillian Smith was dedicated to binding up wounds, to setting free the captives and to bringing healing to the broken.

RR

Worship Resource

Litany

One: I dream of a world that is free
             Of captive people, of oppression,
             That healing may be for all
             . . . But I am only one.

Two: I dream of bringing good tidings
             Of change both possible and real
             That the world's poor may know hope
             . . . But I am only one.

Three: I dream of binding up the brokenhearted
             Those whose spirits have been destroyed
             In the struggle that never ends
             . . . But I am only one

Four: I dream of opening prison doors
             And freeing those so tightly bound
             By prejudice, fear and hate
             . . . But I am only one.

Together: I am only one
             But with you
             And other sisters who care
             We are many.
             Let us go forth together
             With the Spirit of our God
             Upon us all
             And fulfill our dreams.

RR

Prayer

Open my eyes, O God of judgment and compassion,
Let me discern with clarity
That which breaks and that which heals.
Open my ears, O God who hears the pain
And cries of your hurting children
Make me hear as you hear.
Open my heart, O God of love and tenderness,
That I may feel the agony
Of captivity without hope.
Open my mind, O God of knowledge and wisdom,
That I may see truth clearly
And the way to complete healing.
Open my spirit, O patient, impatient God,
That I may have the courage
To speak out and to stand firm.
Cleanse me, O God of purity and truth,
That I may be worthy to respond,
"Here am I, send me."
Amen.

RR

The Raising of Jairus' Daughter

Mark 5:21-24; 35-43

And when Jesus had crossed again in the boat to the other shore, a great crowd gathered about; and Jesus was beside the sea. Then came one of the rulers of the synagogue, Jairus by name, and seeing Jesus, he fell at Jesus' feet, and besought Jesus, saying, "My little daughter is at the point of death. Come lay your hands on her, so that she may be made well, and live." And Jesus went with Jairus . . .

Some people came from the ruler's house who said, "Your daughter is dead. Why trouble the teacher any further?" But, ignoring what they said, Jesus said to the ruler of the synagogue, "Do not fear. Only believe." And Jesus allowed no one to go along except Peter and James and John the brother of James. When they came to the house of the ruler of the synagogue, Jesus saw a tumult, and people weeping and wailing loudly. And when Jesus entered and said to them, "Why do you make this tumult and weep? The child is not dead but sleeping," they laughed at Jesus.

But Jesus put them all outside and took the child's mother and father and Peter, James and John, and went in where the child was. Taking her by the hand, Jesus said to her, "Talitha Cumi," which means, "Little girl, I say to you, arise." And immediately the girl got up and walked; for she was twelve years old. And immediately they were overcome with amazement. And Jesus strictly charged them that no one should know this and told them to give her something to eat.

RSV adapted

Biblical Interpretation

How It Might Have Been

Jairus knelt in desperate prayer. His lovely young daughter Deborah, who was as dear to him as his sons, and who had just officially become a woman, was wasting away with fever. The poultices and potions Dorcas, his wife, had tried, had done no good. Already friends and relatives and mourners for hire had gathered—like vultures, Jairus thought.

He had cautiously asked questions about this new young Rabbi and Healer, named Jesus, whom he had heard about. He had learned where Jesus was likely to be, but no male relative would consent to go in search of the Healer, and he did not care to order a servant to go. Already his aunt Miriam had torn her garments and the flute players were gathered with the professional mourners ready to begin the unholy din with which the Jews greeted death.

Wearily he turned to Dorcas, who shook her head. Deborah was no better. Jairus could hear her struggle for breath. Unable to bear any more, Jairus flung himself out of the house. Perhaps it was beneath his dignity, but he would go to Jesus himself. He hurried toward the last place Jesus had been reported. Of course the people gathered outside his house had tried to stop Jairus, and a few had snickered at the idea of a synagogue ruler, sworn to bar Jesus from speaking in the synagogue, asking Jesus' help. But he had to do something!

When he found Jesus, a crowd surrounded the Healer. Jairus threw himself prostrate at Jesus' feet and cried, "My little daughter is dying. Come and touch her and make her well." And Jesus came.

Before they could get to the house, some of the hangers-on at Jairus' home came—as much in malice as in sorrow—to tell Jairus not to bother the Teacher further because his Deborah was dead. But Jesus turned to Jairus and said, "Don't be afraid. Only believe." And Jesus took three disciples and Jairus and told the rest not to come.

By the time they reached Jairus' home, all his relatives had rent their garments. They and the official mourners were wailing, beating their breasts and pulling their hair. Half a dozen flute players had started on a dirge—the noise was terrible.

"Why are making such a noise and crying so? The child is not dead. She is sleeping," Jesus said. But the crowd laughed and continued their noise. Jesus put them out of the house and took Dorcas and Jairus and the three disciples into the bedroom. Jesus took Deborah's hand and said gently, "Little girl, get up." And Deborah stood up and walked.

Jairus and Dorcas might never stand so tall in the community or the synagogue as they had before, but their cherished daughter had been restored to life and health by the quiet young Healer called Jesus who reached out to heal the broken.

BJB

Literary Interpretation

Jairus' Daughter

"Sweet child lying
   on your narrow virgin cot
   with glassy eyes and temples hot,
     dying,"

"What can I, your father, do?
   If the other elders knew
   What I've thought of trying,
     They'd rather see you dying!

Jairus, sighing,
   "One who's barred from synagogue,
   Cursed as rebel demagogue
     trying

"To lead the people all astray
   down some different 'narrow way'—
   can all those folk be lying
     who say Jesus heals the dying?"

Jairus crying,
   "Jesus free me from this hell,
   make my little daughter well,"
    vying

With the others crowded round
   while the stern disciples frowned.
   But Jesus was replying,
    "Have faith. She is not dying."

Mourners crying.
   "Leave us," Jesus told them all.
   Turned to the child beneath her pall,
    death denying,

Gently saying, "Child arise.
   It is not time for paradise."
   So cease your sighing
    God's love saves us from dying.

BJB

Personal Reflection

Radical surgery once and yet again had not stopped the advance of cancer, but at Thanksgiving time she talked optimistically about the new procedure the doctors were trying—chemotherapy (At that time chemotherapy was very experimental, used only when all else failed.) She felt better. She was so grateful for this break-through. She even spoke of returning to the hospital after she was well to work with other people who had cancer. We promised to come back at Christmas time and bring her father.

On Christmas Eve she could barely come to the table. She had to be fed. Cancer had invaded much of her body and was climbing up her spine. She cried to her husband like a small child, "Georgie, it hurts." And her two year old nephew looked at the grown ups as if

147

to say, "Why don't you make the pain go away?" Her conversation was hardly coherent, but she recognized her father, and "Georgie" finally located the doctor for another prescription. So when we went to bed she was in less pain.

At 2:00 a.m. on Christmas morning her husband woke us to tell us she was dead. She was whole and out of pain again. I do not believe that God wills death for us, but I believe there are times when death is the best and only healer left to us, when death is indeed release and healing. In this case it seemed to us that Jesus had reached out once more to heal the broken.

BJB

Biblical Character

based on Luke 13:10-17

The Crooked Woman

For eighteen years she had been bent double. For eighteen years she had struggled to keep up with her cooking and housework, her gardening and shopping with her back bent and her balance uncertain. For eighteen years she had no chance really to look at her children or grandchildren or to see the stars or the scudding clouds. For eighteen years she had been unable actually to see the teachers at the synagogue or the guest rabbis as they spoke on the sabbath or read from the sacred scrolls.

Now, on this one sabbath day, her whole world was turned upside down—or right side up. Jesus, that controversial young rabbi whom the synagogue leaders were beginning to oppose, was at the synagogue teaching. And called for her—a woman—to come to the men's part of the synagogue. Jesus spoke to her politely, with a respect she had seldom received before. "Madam," Jesus said, "you are healed."

And Jesus touched her. The synagogue leaders said her infirmity was caused by demons who dwelt within her because of some sin. They would not touch her lest they be defiled. But Jesus touched her and she was healed.

The synagogue leaders scolded because Jesus worked on the sabbath but Jesus said, "Do you not untie your ox or your donkey and take it to water on the sabbath? And this woman, this daughter of Abraham, should she remain bound on the sabbath and not be freed from her affliction?"

Jesus called her a daughter of Abraham! Never had she been so acknowledged and honored. Only men were generally so esteemed as to be addressed as descendants of Abraham. Jesus brought back her self esteem as well as her health as he once more reached out to heal the broken.

BJB

Historical Character

Elizabeth Blackwell

Elizabeth Blackwell, known as the first woman doctor of medicine, was fortunate in her father. He thought his daughters as intelligent and as worth educating as his sons. She was fortunate in the time she lived, for voices were being raised in defense of women's rights. But she had to apply to twenty-nine medical schools before one accepted her and that an accident. The faculty put the onus of refusing her application on the student body. And they, as a lark, approved her application. That may have been the last time she was so easily accepted. Even after she completed her degree and took extra work in Paris and London, she was refused an opportunity to work in the New York Dispensary and had to start her own. In the poorest part of New York City it still took time for people to become desperate enough to seek help from the "little doctress."

Despite continuing opposition, Elizabeth Blackwell established a hospital, a medical college and a nursing program. She began a sex education program for young women that was years ahead of her time. She started a prevention program including a "sanitary visitor" long before district nurses and public health workers were considered. She offered her patients dignity as well as medical service as she reached out to heal the broken.

BJB

Worship Resource

Children's Story

If somebody you know is being mean to you, sometimes it seems to rub off on the rest of their family. It shouldn't. But sometimes it's hard to be nice to a friend's little sister or brother when the friend isn't being nice to you. Did you listen carefully when the scripture about Jairus and his daughter and Jesus was read? If you did, you see how Jesus would have you act in such situations.

Jairus was a synagogue or church leader. In his job he had probably refused to invite Jesus to speak at the synagogue when Jesus came to his town. At that time, any traveling preacher was asked to help out with the worship service. But many of the church leaders had gotten together and agreed that Jesus wanted to change too many things, so they wouldn't let him speak.

Then Jairus' little daughter got very sick. None of the doctors he called in could help her. All his friends and relatives had given up and were gathered around to begin the official mourning that was a custom at that time.

When someone dies in our community, we take food to the family, and send flowers or money for some special project the family decides on as a way to remember their loved one who died. We hug members of the family and cry with them quietly and share our pleasant memories of the person who died. But in Jesus' time, people tore their clothes, put ashes on their heads and wailed in a loud voice to show their sorrow and sympathy. And that's what Jairus' friends were getting ready to do.

But Jairus wasn't ready to let his little daughter die. In spite of the fact that he hadn't been too nice to Jesus, he went to Jesus—that would take courage, wouldn't it—and asked Jesus to come and make his daughter well.

And Jesus came! He didn't say, "But, why should I help you, you didn't help me?" He came, and he told the noisy, wailing people to stop mourning—that's one word for being sorry about somebody's death—and he brought the little girl back to health. Jesus was willing to heal the sick even when their families hadn't been nice to him.

Are we willing to be nice to friends and their families even when we don't think they've been nice to us? We need to ask for Jesus' help so we can be.

BJB

Prayer

We come broken, tattered, soiled by our week in the world. Renew us, cleanse us, bind up our wounds, O God, our Rock and our Redeemer.

O God, we thank you for this new day, for this time that we can come to you for healing and renewal.

We thank you for those material and spiritual blessings we have received.

We thank you for the strength and help we receive from you and from friends in your church when we lose our livelihood, our loved ones, our health.

151

We thank you for this church and this
church family, and pray for its
continued growth and strength.

We pray for your guidance to
us as individuals;
as a church;
as a country;
as a world.

Now we pray for your blessing on the
service that we may live in such
a way that we, like Jesus, will
live to heal the broken.

In Jesus' name. Amen.

BJB

The Woman at The Well

John 4:7-18; 24-26, 39

Jesus had to pass through Samaria. So Jesus came to a city of Samaria called Sychar, near the field that Jacob gave to his son Joseph. The well of Jacob, Leah and Rachel was there, and so Jesus, wearied with the journey, sat down beside the well. It was about the sixth hour.

There came a woman of Samaria to draw water. Jesus said to her, "Give me a drink." For the disciples had gone into the city to buy food. The Samaritan woman said to Jesus, "How is it that you, a Jew, ask a drink of me, a woman of Samaria?" For the Jews have no dealings with Samaritans. Jesus answered her, "If you knew the gift of God, and who it is that is saying to you, 'Give me a drink,' you would have asked me and I would have given you living water." The woman said to Jesus, "Teacher, you have nothing to draw with, and the well is deep; where do you get that living water? Are you greater than our ancestors Jacob, Leah and Rachel, who gave us this well, and drank from it themselves, and their children and livestock?" Jesus said to her, "Everyone who drinks of this water will thirst again, but whoever drinks of the water that I shall give them will never thirst; the water that I shall give them will become to them a spring of water welling up to eternal life." The woman said to Jesus, "Teacher, give me this water, that I may not thirst, nor come here to draw."

Jesus said to her, "Go, call your husband and come here." The woman answered Jesus, "I have no husband." Jesus said to her, "You are right in saying, 'I have no husband'; for you have had five husbands, and he whom you now have is not your husband; this you said truly." The woman said to Jesus, "Teacher, I perceive that you are a prophet. Our ancestors worshiped on this mountain; and you say that in Jerusalem is the place where people ought to worship." Jesus said to her, "Woman, believe me, the hour is coming when neither on this mountain or

153

in Jerusalem will you worship the Creator. You worship what you do not know; we worship what we know, for salvation is from the Jews. But the hour is coming, and now is, when the true worshipers will worship the Creator in spirit and truth, for such the Creator seeks as worshipers. God is spirit, and those who worship God must worship in spirit and truth." The woman said to Jesus, "I know that Messiah is coming (the one called the Christ); when the Messiah comes we will be shown all things." Jesus said to her, "I who speak to you am the Messiah."

Just then the disciples returned. They marveled that Jesus was talking with a woman, but none said, "What do you wish?" or "Why are you talking with her?" So the woman left her water jar, and went away into the city, and said to the people, "Come see a person who told me all that I ever did. Can this be the Christ?" . . .

Many Samaritans from that city believed in Jesus because of the woman's testimony, "Jesus told me all that I ever did."

RSV adapted

Biblical Interpretation

Only John tells us of the encounter of Jesus and the Samaritan woman. His purpose was to present her as "living water." Jesus and the disciples were on their way to Galilee and, against the established habit of the people, Jesus wished to stop at Samaria, which was a place people hated because of its religious and cultural mixture. Jesus wished to save the repudiated woman and her neighbours. God's grace and love are big.

Let's see some details of the biblical passage:

1. Jacob's well—According to tradition, the well was made by the patriarch Jacob, and, therefore, the historical and religious connection was very strong.
2. Jesus, the incarnated God, has limitations and therefore is thirsty.

3. Jesus, the incarnated God, is humiliated—because of thirst Jesus asked a woman for water. She happened to be an enemy of the Jews.
4. Jesus, the incarnated God, has become known—because of the woman's amazement and denial, Jesus tells her that as the Messiah, *Jesus is the provider of the living water.*
5. The true place for adoration—Jesus decentralizes the place for adoration for the Jews and the Samaritans by telling them the time had come to adore God "in spirit and in truth."
6. Jesus is identified as the Messiah—This is the climax of the encounter of Jesus with the Samaritan woman, who in light of the testimony of what "she had done" left immediately leaving her water pitcher, and told the people what Jesus had told her. She introduced Jesus as the Messiah. As the result of this testimony, a nation accepted Jesus as their Messiah.

OS

Literary Interpretation

Symbolisms—John 4:7-26

Trip
Tired
Draw Water
To try among ourselves
Water of life
Well
To be thirsty
Gift of God
Water—fountain of eternal life
Truth
God is Spirit
Messiah
I am

OS

Personal Reflection

Because of my husband's work with the Biblical Society, we used to visit churches in different denominations. Those visits were very enriching because of all the people I met and because I learned different ways to worship.

During that time I met a beautiful woman. This woman had been a "Samaritan" before she knew Jesus—she had had five "husbands." It was very difficult for her to be seen as "a new creature." Many churches and their pastors could not accept her past life, but God's work had transformed her and she was faithful to Jesus, her Saviour.

I met her in her church during an evangelization course. She showed a lot of interest in our teachings, and when it was time to go out to testify and distribute the Scriptures, she was one of the first persons who brought her daughter and granddaughter to the church.

When I read the passage of the Samaritan woman, I remembered this woman in my country who in the same way had found Jesus as her Saviour. There had been a pastor who did not look into her past, but into her present and future, and told her about God's love. The pastor rescued her for a fruitful life in a society where even her name was disliked. This is the love of God, marvelous and abundant for all those who thirst for new life, for all those who are not satisfied with their sinful life. God is love.

OS

Biblical Character

John 4:7-18; 24-26

Jesus and the Samaritan Woman

Jesus did not necessarily have to go through Samaria, since there was another path that went around it, but out of love and piety Christ had an appointment with a poor woman of that region. Which of us will be willing to have contact with a woman of uncertain reputation? What will be our attitude towards a woman like the Samaritan? Jesus broke all the canons to share with the Samaritan "the water of life."

The woman questioned Jesus' request for water. No one from the Orient would have denied Jesus such a favor if the fight among the two nations had not existed. To what extent do we allow ourselves to be influenced by other people and cultures because of historic actions? How should the church struggle against that and against discrimination?

Another very important aspect of the Samaritan woman was that even though she had weak moral beliefs, she had a very deep sense of religion and was waiting for the "Messiah." What impelled her to immorality we do not know, but we know that Jesus felt she was a sincere person who sought God, and Jesus helped her find "the fountain of eternal life." Do we judge people by their appearance or are we careful enough to find out first who they really are? Do we have the authority to judge them?

The conclusion of this drama occurs when the woman found a new horizon when she accepted from Jesus "the water of life" and, leaving her water pitcher behind, went to the city to tell about what had happened.

Have we been converted and felt the joy and liberation that she experienced? And what have we done with that blessing?

When she told the people of her encounter with Jesus they wanted to know and to talk with Jesus personally. They discovered for themselves that Jesus was the Messiah. When you testify about Jesus other people also want to know the Christ.

OS

Historical Application

Because of her religious and racial beliefs, the encounter between Jesus and the Samaritan woman was violent.

The Jews more than the Samaritans, hated the people of Samaria because they had physical contact with other nations. The story began in 722 BC when the Assyrians subdued the Israelites and took them to Assyria as slaves. (2 Kings 17:24).

The foreigners who were placed in Samaria by the Assyrians mingled with the remnant who were not transported. Since these people who came from Babylon, Cuthah, Avva, Hamath and Sephar-va'im did not "know the law of the god of the land" the king of Assyria had one of the transported priests returned to teach them (2 Kings 17:27-29). In time mixed marriages took place between Jews and Gentiles.

When the main body of Jews came back from exile, the Samaritans offered them help to reconstruct the temple in Jerusalem, but the Jews did not accept their offer (Esdras 4:1-4). This caused mutual resentment since the Samaritans were offended because their help was not accepted; and the Jews were offended because the Samaritan Jews had not kept their faith in Jehovah, and because they stopped the earlier reconstruction of the temple in Jerusalem.

As centuries went by, the hate among Jews and Samaritans increased to such an extent that when the Jews had to go to the north, they went around the Jordan so as not to "contaminate" themselves with the people of Samaria. The worst insult for a Jew was to be called a Samaritan. It is recorded in John 8:48-49 that Jesus was accused of being a Samaritan.

Sometimes history gives us good memories and valuable lessons, but other times the memories are negative which can divide and destroy nations. What should be the yardstick for Christians to measure their behaviour in the world?

OS

Worship Resource

Litany

Right: Give us living water
Left: So that we never thirst again.
Right: Let us treat each other like sisters and brothers in Christ
Left: So that we never thirst again.
Right: Let us know God's gift.
Left: So that we can share your salvation.
Right: Give us the water of life.
Left: So that we can share it with those who thirst.
Right: Give us water from the fountain
Left: Water for eternal life.
Right: Grant us life in your Spirit
Left: So that we can free ourselves.
Right: Let us truly adore you
Left: For the salvation of our fellow creatures.
Right: Speak with us, Jesus
Left: So that we know all your truth.
All: Thank you God for you are the fresh water of eternal life.
Amen.

OS

Prayer

God, we thank you because you came to find and saved what was lost. We thank you because you make no exceptions of people, and saved the Samaritan woman when everybody else has rejected her.

Grant us, God, that we too, have compassion not only for women but also for men who have prostituted themselves.

Forgive us God, because many times we don't want to know anything about the "Samaritan woman" who lives close to us or whom we know. Help us understand that we are not better than the Samaritan woman, but that your grace has redeemed us and has put us in a privileged position.

Thank you, God, because with your example and gospel of love you impel us to seek and redeem the many Samaritan women and men of our neighborhood.

Thank you, God, for your mercy and your excellence. In Jesus Christ, Amen.

OS

The Healing Touch

Luke 8:43-48

And a woman who had a flow of blood for twelve years and could not be healed by any one, came up behind Jesus, and touched the hem of Jesus' garment; and immediately her flow of blood ceased. And Jesus said, "Who was it that touched me?" When all denied it, Peter said, "Leader, the multitudes surround you and press upon you!" But Jesus said, "Someone touched me; for I perceive that power has gone forth from me." And when the woman saw that she was not hidden, she came trembling, and falling down before Jesus declared in the presence of all the people why she had touched Jesus, and how she had been immediately healed. And Jesus said to her, "Daughter, your faith has made you well; go in peace."

(RSV adapted)

Biblical Interpretation

In the Lukan passage (as well as in its parallel sources, Matthew 9:20 ff. and Mark 5:25 ff.) we see Jesus as the Great Physician. The one who brings the age of salvation is also the mighty healer. And even though Christ's healing ministry often means conflict with local authorities, popular opinion recognizes that even a touch of the healer's garment means cure. Contact between Jesus and a sick person always means total health or wholeness, even if the individual has been sick from birth, or for many years, as in the instance of this woman with a 12 year long hemorrhage.

Jewish laws uphold her total "uncleanness" (Leviticus 12 and 15 record so-called health and dietary laws in depth). According to the stated custom, a woman is "unclean" during the menstrual period, for one week thereafter, seven days after giving birth to a boy, 14 days after giving birth to a girl, with an additional "purification period" during which she may not enter the worship area. Not until the priest makes a sin offering on her behalf (Leviticus 15:30) is the woman made "clean" again. For the woman in the Lukan account, community rejection is certain and unquestioned; to touch her is to contaminate oneself. Hence, the " 'good' Jewish male was expected to say to such a woman as the one with the 12 year flow of blood, 'Begone, thou filthy woman!' " (*Jesus According to Woman*, Wahlberg, p. 34).

Both the woman and Jesus take actions which shock the onlooking community. On her part, this unnamed female audaciously risks *touching* a Jewish male, with the hope of Jesus' reputed power to heal. She realizes the extent of her bold action and, when the group recognizes her presence, immediately trembles in fear and resumes her "appropriate" social place, falling to her knees. For Jesus to speak with and to heal this distressed woman is a behavior contradicting, and virtually overturning, the ancient Jewish system, a system which Jesus certainly understands, using its language of connecting a person's physical suffering with their own sin. "Daughter, your *faith* has made you well . . ."

JLH

Literary Interpretation

Wholeness

Blood
Outcast
All Alone
Unclean! Unclean!
No hope for healing

Touch
Jesus
Blood ceases
Trembling! Falling!
I think I am healed

Faith
Daughter
Go in peace
Jesus heals; Jesus loves!
Whole person of God

JLH

Personal Reflection

Whenever I faithfully administer the elements of communion in a eucharist service, when I distribute the symbols of bread/body and wine/blood, I can think of my New Testament sister with the long flow of blood, and I smile to myself, saying "Thank God!" What the power of God healed for her years ago, the power of God sustains for me today—a feeling of worthiness and "appropriateness" at the highest level, no matter what the onlooking community says to me.

It is then with rightful pride, and no shame, that I answer my young daughter's curious questions every month. "Yes, sweetie, it's o.k. that Mommy bleeds; no, it doesn't hurt very much. Yes, you will too someday, so you can have a baby if you want; that's how God made us." Maybe by the time her cycle of creation's reminder begins, she will feel more "o.k." about her body and her sex than have the generations of women before her.

Because I, too, in my own circles of life experiences have felt some of the rejection, the untouchable-ness, the discrimination by males in power, as did the woman at Jesus' feet. Magazine and newspaper articles and local clergy groups continue the unending male references to pastor, and I feel like a nonperson. Some people refuse to accept reality and appear simply unable to comprehend that I am more than the Reverend's wife. But I am also a bit of the "audacious" nature and will reach out in the hope that eventually our touch of one another makes us all whole persons.

JLH

Biblical Character

Mark 10:46ff

Bartimaus

Bartimaus, the blind beggar, is another New Testament character whose audacious faith in Jesus' ability to heal parallels the woman with the flow of blood. He, too, is scorned by others, both because of his physical limitation and because of his determination to encounter the Christ. In fact, the more they scold, the louder he shouts, until Jesus intervenes on his behalf. In a direct confrontation, the One of God asks a pointed question—"What do you want me to do for you?" Following the beggar's obvious plea for sight, his request is granted on the basis of his faith. Although the Biblical record is indefinite regarding the future, it does say the man "followed [Jesus] along the road" (Jerusalem Bible). Is the blind man's *thanks* his willingness to become a disciple?

The beggar's story, along with the account of the bleeding woman, may provide several questions for us. What is our physical or emotional limitation? Do we acknowledge that God has the power to remove such an obstacle, or to make us functioning, whole people in spite of it? If the Divine asked us personally, "What do you want me to do for you?" how would we respond? How would it feel to be the "object" of a miracle, or what *is* the miracle in our life? What is the strength of our faith? How specifically do we express our gratitude or hope for what is given us?

A blind beggar, an "unclean" woman, a timid indivual, a fearful person, myself—all loved and healed by the One who originally grants life to all.

JLH

Historical Character

Sarah Righter Major

In about 1826 when she was eighteen, Sarah Righter felt called of God to preach. There were no women ministers in the Church of the Brethren at that time. In fact, it was 85 years before the first woman, Mattie Cunningham Dolby, a black woman, was installed as a minister. And in 1917 Mattie Dolby was actually shut out of the church by being invited by one congregation to find a place closer home to worship since her family was no longer welcome as they had been. It was, therefore, not surprising that Sarah Righter did not act upon her calling at once.

Her father, Peter Keyser, a minister in Philadelphia, and Israel Paulsen of the Amwell, New Jersey congregation encouraged her, but the 1834 yearly meeting ruled:

concerning a sister's preaching: not approved of:
considered such sister in danger, not only [of]
exposing her own state of grace to temptation, but
also causing temptation, discord, and disputes among
other members.

A committee of elders failed to enforce the annual meeting's decision. But they did not give her official permission to preach either. As one member of the committee said, "I could not give my vote to silence someone who can outpreach me." Henceforth Sarah Righter could preach if asked but could not volunteer.

After her marriage to Thomas Major, a minister, she and her husband witnessed together. Generally he would open the service and then invite his wife up from her seat in the congregation to speak. Although she continued to minister to individuals, in jails and hospitals, and was known for her care for black people, she could speak in churches only when invited. She was not accepted by her denomination. The meeting thought she was a danger to herself and others, as the religious authorities of Jesus' day thought of the woman with the flow of blood.

But God accepted and used Sarah Righter Major's gift, as Jesus accepted the woman's faith. And both were blessed despite the mores of their day.

BJB

165

Worship Resource

Litany

Left: From the pain of exclusion from Thy church
Right: Thou, O God, dost deliver us.
Left: From rejection of the gifts we would offer on thy altar
Right: Thou, O God, dost deliver us.
Left: From being considered less valuable, more sinful, because
        we are women
Right: Thou, O God, dost deliver us.
Left: Thou dost send thy loving, caring word
Right: To draw the circle of the church large enough to include
        everyone.
Left: Thou dost send thy loving, caring word
Right: To accept our gifts even when they are not traditional.
Left: Thou dost send they loving, caring word
Right: To free all people—women and men—from sin and value-
        lessness.
All: Thou, O God, dost deliver us.
(note: users may wish to change the language into more contemporary pronouns and verb forms.)

BJB

Prayer

O God, sometimes I wonder—if I look in the mirror, will I see a
    reflection?
When I offered to preach, the answer came, "concerning a sister's
    preaching: not approved of . . ."—no one saw me.
Even when I was finally installed as a minister, I was soon told "to
    find a place of worship closer home"—no one would hear me.
When I came to the temple, I was sent away. I was unclean because
    I was a woman who had "a flow of blood." No one dared touch me.

O God, if I look in the mirror, will there be a reflection? Will you see me, hear me, touch me, heal me?

O God, when the world turns me into a nonperson, I thank you for sending your word made flesh to the broken, the oppressed, the ignored.

I thank you for the Messiah who asked women to witness to your saving love, who refused to consider women evil because some of their bodily functions differed from men, who *saw* people regardless of sex or ethnic or religious background, who reached out to touch and be touched.

I thank you that though I may not see my reflection in the eyes of the world, I am reflected in your eyes as a valued disciple. I am there, I am seen, heard, touched.

Thank you, O God. May it be so. Amen.

BJB

Would That You Knew The Things That Make For Peace

Justice, Righteousness and Peace

Isaiah 32:16-20

Then justice will dwell in the wilderness,
  and righteousness abide in the fruitful field.
And the effect of righteousness will be peace,
  and the result of righteousness, quietness and trust forever.
My people will abide in a peaceful habitation,
  in secure dwellings, and in quiet resting places.
And the forest will utterly go down,
  and the city will be utterly laid low.
Happy are you who sow beside all waters,
  who let the feet of the ox and ass range free.

RSV

Biblical Interpretation

This passage follows a call to mourning issued to the rich women of Judah who are to weep for the imminent devastation of their country (v. 9-14). The word of violence gives way to an idyllic portrait of a peaceful future that will begin with an outpouring of God's Spirit upon the people and the land (v. 15).

The prophet poetically depicts the results of the Spirit outpouring. The territory will be known as a place of peace and justice. The people will work to uphold that reputation and will find their reward in a calm confidence that militaristic people never know. They will feel secure in their way of life, live safely in their homes and sleep undisturbed in their graves.

Verse 19 presents a problem in that it jars the overall tranquility of the passage with its harshness. This leads some commentators to believe that it rightly belongs after verse 14. Others choose to leave it in place and interpret it to mean that once Judah's enemies are judged (symbolized by hail) and destroyed (when the forest comes down), Judah can build her cities on the plain rather than as fortresses high in the rocks. Then the farmers will be able to plant without concern for protection and can allow their animals to range freely for feed.

This passage speaks to us of a society characterized by the peaceful stance of its citizens. The emphasis is on the peacefulness of spirit that belongs to those who rely on God, not arms for protection.

JG

Literary Interpretation

After the Rain

The rain ran clear today
Dousing trees, drenching ground.
 I caught
 In up-turned hands
 This essential ingredient,
 This liquid of life that greens my world.

Once I saw a child's drawing.
It was called: "Black Rain."
 She drew
 About a day when a mushroom grew in the sky
 And the rain ran black.

No "once upon a time," story this,
No dream of childish imagination.

Did that rain
Mark the palms that caught it
With the stigmata of the crucified?
  After that rain
  What color was the world?

JG

Personal Reflection

Whenever I read scripture that describes how life will be characterized in the Realm of God I am struck with the dream-like qualities of these texts. I feel myself lulled by the beauty of the images . . . peaceful pastures . . . fertile fields . . . undisturbed beds and graves. This is the stuff of dreams and visions—the world we would all love to create. But it is not the world we know.

Our world is one of war and terror, poverty and injustice where the few enjoy too much at the expense of the many who go without what is necessary for survival. Our world is one of bombings and assassinations, starvation and human rights violations. It is not the pretty world where there is "quietness and trust."

I ask myself: "What does this scripture have to offer me? How does it meet me in my world?" The only answer I know is that this passage expresses God's deepest desire for this world. As such, it must be my deepest desire too—and the vision toward which I must work.

One of the "things that make for peace" is a vision of peace. This vision has been handed down to me by the mothers and fathers of faith. It is for me to carry into this generation. It is for me to bring to the "real world" . . . until no one can tell the difference between the world and the vision.

JG

Biblical Character

Esther

At first it would seem incongrous to select Esther as an example of one who worked for peace. The Book of Esther ends in violence and bloodshed partly due to Esther's political intervention on behalf of her people. Yet, the Book of Esther expresses a belief that many in our generation hold as true—peace through strength.

There are some who would disagree with this stance and regard it as an unacceptable means of bringing about peace. The reality, however, is this: we are a people caught between the world as it is and the world as it should be. God's dream of a world filled with justice, righteousness and peace will not be realized if we do not act according to individual conscience.

Esther was a woman who found herself in a position of influence at a time when the Jewish people were threatened with destruction. At the risk of her own life she used what little political power she had to create a situation wherein her people could defend themselves against their enemies. We may not agree with the means by which peace was obtained, but the point is that Esther acted.

It is difficult to decide simply what it is that makes for peace. What seems obvious, however, is that we are called to be instruments of peace—imperfect as we are.

JG

Historical Character

Dorothy Day

Dorothy Day is one of the finer examples of a woman in our own time who lived to bring the vision of universal justice and peace closer to a reality. Her life displayed a wedding of faith and action. She set herself staunchly against all war and participation in war. She lived with a strong sense of personal responsibility for her neighbor and gave her life to achieve a measure of justice for the poor. She saw Christ in every destitute person she encountered and felt compelled to respond to that image. The unwanted were not to be shunned, but embraced.

This was a woman who chose faith at a great price, for in choosing God she lost the man she loved most—a man who, despite his love for her and their daughter, could not accept her decision to live for God. She was a woman who went against her own desires, conscious that the God who pursued her would be satisfied with nothing less than all.

Founder of the Catholic Worker Movement, Dorothy Day lived in voluntary poverty—a lifestyle that gave that movement high credibility. The Movement featured houses of hospitality opened to the homeless, communal living, and farming. In 1933 she began publishing *The Catholic Worker*, a newspaper that became the voice of the Movement. The primary emphasis of the Movement was on hard work, simple living, and nonviolent action to promote social justice.

Dorothy Day, like her numerous associates, was a woman who stood in the "gap" between God's dream for society and reality with which we live. In her being, and that of the many like her, the two worlds moved closer together.

JG

Worship Resource

Responsive Reading #66

Congregational Benediction

Leader: God calls us to bring justice to the wilderness that is our world.

People: We will answer God's call for justice.

Leader: God's desire is for righteousness in our fields.

People: We will work to accomplish God's desire.

Leader: God's dream is for peace in our pastures.

People: We commit ourselves to dream God's dream.

Leader: And the fruits of justice, righteousness and peace will be quietness and confidence forever.

People: And the promise is that we will live in secure homes and sleep in undisturbed graves.

All: WE WILL GO NOW EACH TO OUR SEPARATE WORLD UNITED BY THE GOD WE LOVE AND THE DREAM WE CARRY. AMEN

Hymn 323

JG

Prayer

God of Justice, you have said: "Then justice will dwell in the wilderness . . ." I am compelled to ask: *when* will justice dwell in the wildernesses of my world?

God of Righteousness, you have said that "righteousness will abide in the fertile fields." I wonder *how* will that righteousness come about?

God of Peace, you have said: "Then my people will live in peaceful pastures . . ." Again I must ask: *when? how long* before the coming of peace to my world?

175

The vision is lovely. The dream feels true. But when I look up from your Book I see the faces of abused children, broken men and frightened women. I see the bloated stomachs of starving people, the jaded expressions of war veterans, the ashy brown color that mixes in with the blue of city skies. Pain. Fear. Hunger. Hopelessness. Pollution. I see all of these and the vision recedes.

I confess to you my discouragement and my disbelief. I ask again that you teach me the things that make for peace. Rekindle the vision within me. I seek to be a dreamer for peace, a woman for justice. Amen.

JG

Blessed Are The Peacemakers

Matthew 5:9

"Blessed are the peacemakers, for they shall be called children of God."

RSV adapted

Biblical Interpretation

I attended a parade in Belfast. The parade was to commemorate a time when Catholics in Northern Ireland could be arrested without a warrant and be held for an indefinite amount of time. This was in the early 1970's when the IRA had just a few members, and only a few weapons. On the day of the parade I attended, the army and police surrounded the area; they appeared to be ready to fire their machine guns. When at one point children started throwing stones at the police from a roof top, the police started to shoot plastic bullets into the crowd. Perhaps if I had not been there, and had not been shot at, I could go on ignoring the need for peace in our violent and brutal society. It's sad that it takes more than Jesus saying, "Blessed are the peacemakers, for they shall be called children of God," to motivate us to work for peace.

In Matthew, Jesus tells us no longer is it an "eye for an eye and a tooth for a tooth." If your sister strikes you on one cheek, turn the other cheek. If your brother forces you to carry his bag one mile, carry it a second mile also. No longer can we love only those who love us, but we must love our enemies.

However, this does not mean that we should passively accept injustice. Jesus was not passive when knocking over the tables of the money changers and the benches of those selling doves. And even when the chief priest and the teachers were indignant about the children shouting "Hosanna to the Child of David," Jesus wasn't apologetic. Jesus retorted, "Have you never read, 'from the lips of children and infants you have ordained praise?' "

Perhaps the closest we can come to understanding this kind of peacemaking is through the life of Dr. Martin Luther King, Jr., who said:

> The ultimate weakness of violence is that it is a descending spiral, begetting the very thing it seeks to destroy. Instead of diminishing evil, it multiplies it. Through violence, you may murder the liar, but you cannot murder the lie, nor establish the truth. Through violence you can murder the hater but you do not murder the hate. In fact, violence merely increases the hate . . . Returning violence for violence multiplies violence, adding darkness to a night already devoid of stars. Darkness cannot drive out darkness; only light can do that. Hate cannot drive out hate: only love can do that. (from Fellowship of Reconcilation poster)

And as Jesus died carrying the cross a second mile, Martin Luther King, Jr., died trying to love somebody, trying to be right on the war question, and trying to love and serve humanity.

But let us not forget the children shouting "Hosanna" for Jesus. Too often we forget the quiet peacemakers in the Bible and in our present world. O, "Blessed are the peacemakers, for they shall be called children of God."

PG-K

Literary Interpretation

Our Mother God

1. God, like a mother, sits beside her sobbing child at night, who's
    afraid of the dark, and of scary things, and of crying all alone
    "Oh baby, it's all right; it's all right, my child.
    Oh baby, it's all right; it's all right, my child."
CHORUS:
> God, our Mother, comfort bringer, protect us in the
> dark. Gently holding, ever guiding, our loving
> Mother God.

2. When all the world seems dark and dreary, and no one seems to
    care
    Though your friends may have gone and you cry alone,
    remember God is still there,
    saying, "It's all right; it's all right, my child.
    Baby it's all right; it's all right, my child."

3. If you fall along life's journey, God is always there.
    And she'll pick you up, and hold you tight,
        and kiss away your teardrops.
    "Oh baby, it's all right; it's all right, my child.
    Baby, it's all right; it's all right, my child.

PG-K

Personal Reflection

It's difficult to think of myself as a peacemaker. At the time of my
writing this I am in Northern Ireland, working for several organizations which work for peace. I'd like to think that when I provide
the opportunity for Protestant children to meet Catholic
children that I am "making peace." But the peacemakers are
really the children; they reconcile themselves to each other.

During my stay in Ireland I took a group of children to Corrymeela, a community of people working for reconciliation in Northern Ireland. At the Corrymeela retreat center in Ballycastle, groups of prisoners' families, single parents, and children come and share a week together during the summer or a few days together some time throughout the rest of the year. The children I took to Corrymeela were Catholic and Protestant children from troubled areas in Belfast; most of them live along a peace line (a street or wall which separates Protestant and Catholic communities). These areas were worse during the 1970's, but still rioting and stone throwing occur. Most of these children had never been with anybody from the other side; for all they knew, those people were green with tiny horns. So when the children discovered that the "taigs" or the "prods" (slang words which mean Catholic and Protestant) looked like them, talked like them, and even liked to play the same games, the children began to accept one another. They played together, ate together, and even by choice, slept together. By the end of the week it was impossible to see any division between them, other than those caused by personality conflicts.

Needless to say, it was sad to see the children go back to Belfast, to their segregated, working class ghettos. Maybe they can come together again for a day trip and a weekend at Corrymeela, but they won't be able to stay long. We can't change the community they live in; we can only hope, that by their experience at Corrymeela, they will learn to accept each other as they grow into adults. They are the only ones to break down the walls that divide their communities.

PG-K

Biblical Character

based on John 4:1-42

The Samaritan Woman

When this woman of Samaria approached the well, she saw a Jew sitting by it, not Jesus, nor a peacemaker. She didn't expect Jesus to say anything to her; after all Jews considered Samaritans unclean and would not use the same dishes that Samaritans had used. And so, when Jesus asked this woman for a sip of her water, she was very surprised. She could not understand why Jesus would ask her for water, and she didn't understand who Jesus was. It wasn't until Jesus had told her everything she had ever done that she believed Jesus was, in fact, the Messiah.

At that moment, she had a choice to make. She could have chosen to ignore the impact Jesus made upon her life, and say nothing to her friends. She could have chosen not to grasp the opportunity for peacemaking—not to pass on the peacemaking Jesus offered her. But she chose instead to risk telling her friends of Jesus. And it was a risk. She didn't know whether they would be willing to go with her to Jesus; they could have laughed at her instead. She didn't know what their response would be; they could have rejected her because she had spoken to a Jew. Yet she took the risk of being a quiet peacemaker—of becoming a bridge between Jesus and her friends.

And the Samaritan woman's friends followed her to Jesus. After they had listened to Jesus speak they told her, "We no longer believe just because of what you said; now we have heard it for ourselves, and we know this one really is the Saviour of the world." At that moment, this woman of Samaria was probably feeling a freedom she had never felt before. And most likely she was feeling very happy. "Blessed are the peacemakers, they shall be called children of God."

Historical Character

Rosa Parks

Rosa Parks was a quiet peacemaker. She lived in Montgomery, Alabama where she worked as a seamtress in a local department store. She depended on a bus to take her to and from work. At this time, 1955, black passengers were allowed to sit in the back of the buses in Montgomery if there was enough room. If a white person needed a seat, however, the black person was forced to stand. And Rosa was a black woman.

One day, December 1, 1955, Rosa was simply too tired to stand after a long day's work; she refused to get up and give her seat to a white person. So she was arrested and taken to jail for "breaching the peace."

After the arrest of Rosa Parks that day, the bus boycott in Montgomery, Alabama began. Black persons refused to use the buses until the law was changed. Rosa Parks was a quiet peacemaker, a bridge builder for peace and justice among people.

This song was written in memory of Martin Luther King, Jr. who led the bus boycott in Montgomery and later led the struggle for justice for blacks. As you sing "I Am Somebody," remember Rosa Parks' contribution to this peace movement.

I Am Somebody

CHORUS: I AM SOMEBODY, NOT JUST ANYBODY, A STRONG ABLE BODY, I AM.
AND CAUSE I FEEL LIKE SOMEBODY, YOU'RE NOT JUST ANYBODY, A PART OF ONE BODY WE ARE.

1. Dr. King lived down in the heart of Dixie Land, where according to the law,
   on bus rides he should stand.
   He broke this law by sitting down while the white people stood,
   through this he hoped it might be understood. (CHORUS)
2. He spoke of love and of using our might, nonviolently to stand up for our
   equal rights.

He sat in jail, and spoke aloud, saying "I am someone."
And hoped someday we could all live as one. (CHORUS)
3. It seems kind of strange how great humans die,
They're killed by the passion of another person's pride.
He said, "I am black, I am proud, and I'm going to be free."
His life was taken 'cause they thought we would see, that
(CHORUS)

PG-K

Worship Resource

Litany

People: We know no peace.
1 Reader: Our children are taught to mistrust and hate somebody
           because of the color of his skin or her religion.
2 Reader: Our children are taught that men don't cry and that
           women can't be strong and independent.
3 Reader: Our children are taught that they don't know what
           they're talking about, and that older people can't be
           spontaneously funny.
People: We know no peace.
1 Reader: Our children are forced to live with the threat of
           nuclear warfare.
2 Reader: Our children are forced to play only with children from
           their side of the peace line.
People: We know no peace.
3 Reader: Our children in India and Africa die from diseases and
           malnutrition.
1 Reader: Our children in the slum areas of New York or Chicago
           suffer from lack of opportunity; families in our land
           sleep in tents and church basements and alleys.
People: We know no peace.

183

2 Reader: Our children can't speak the same language as other children because they are not allowed to speak with them.

3 Reader: Our children don't know what other children are like, because they are not allowed to play with them.

People: Our children don't know how to love other children, because they are not allowed to love them.

All: God, help us to listen to our children. Help us to cry as they cry when they are feeling hurt. Help us to be like our children, and readily accept the differences in other people. And help us to be like children who freely express their feelings and warmly touch the people around them. Help us, God, to allow our children to go to Jesus and know your peace. Amen.

PG-K

Prayer

Reader: God, we are blinded by hatred, and prejudice, and illusions that peace begins when, and only when, the other person changes. Too often we forget that peace begins within ourselves.

People: God we are blind, help us to see.

Reader: Save us from illusions that peace can begin if another person's rights are taken away.

People: That is not peace; that is a silent oppression which is just as violent as any discrimination.

Reader: Let us speak out against discrimination and work to bring justice to this unjust society.

People: And let us love those who hurt us.

Reader: We remember our mothers and fathers who worked for peace and died seeking peace.

People: They give us strength and courage to continue working for peace, though it often feels like we're wasting our time.

All: O God, help us to bring people together: Catholic and Protestant children in Northern Ireland; blacks and whites in South Africa; Central American leaders and the peasants and farmers in Central America; Western and Eastern Countries; and any majority and minority groups which need to be reconciled.

Reader: Help us to live in the sure knowledge of your love for us and for all persons.

People: Help us to feel like somebody, despite our personal limitations, weaknesses, and experiences. And help us to respect other people.

Reader: Help us to turn to you, O God, in all of life's experiences.

People: Nurture us and guide us as our mothers and fathers may have nurtured us, and protect us as our fathers and mothers may have protected us.

All We want to learn from your peace and grow in your love. For this we pray. Amen.

PGK

My Peace I Give To You

John 14: 27; Luke 19:41-44

"Peace I leave with you; my peace I give to you; not as the world gives do I give to you. Let not your hearts be troubled, neither let them be afraid."

****

And when Jesus drew near and saw the city, Jesus wept over it, saying, "Would that even today you knew the things that make for peace! But now they are hid from your eyes. For the days shall come upon you, when your enemies will cast up a bank about you and surround you, and hem you in on every side, and dash you to the ground, you and your children within you, and they will not leave one stone upon another in you; because you did not know the time of your visitation."

RSV adapted

****

Biblical Interpretation

The concept for peace Jesus uses in these passages is the overflowing of blessings for people and land—the supreme good. The way the world defines peace is different from the way Christ defines peace. The world defines peace as only attainable through force and control. Christ suggests a wholeness and oneness of people and earth. The peace to which Christ refers is not removed from conflict, but the purpose of the conflict is for change rather than for punishment.

186

Christ taught that when one hurts all hurt, when one feels joy all feel joy. All are interconnected. When we recognize this interconnectedness and act on it, we create a oneness, wholeness and ultimately peace. When we experience another's pain and feel with them rather than competing for their attention, we develop the love, closeness and peace to which Christ was referring. We become a blessing to one another. This feeling with, however, involves taking the risk of putting aside, temporarily, one's own concerns in order to hear the other's without judgment. This act of peacemaking requires sometimes undeserved trust and vulnerability. Nations not only have the problem of living the kind of peace Jesus Christ tried to teach us. Individuals in their daily relationships find this a very difficult task. Our human nature wants to win and protect self at all costs, even true happiness. Our human nature finds living in a state of separateness and feeling some sense of power easier to control than living in a state of peace.

CW-H

Literary Interpretation

Based on Luke 19:41-44

Who's Peace

Tension.
Similarities collide.
Parent strikes child
in anger,
wanting control, power,
feeling frustrated, powerless.
Each separate, unheard.
"If you only knew today,
what is needed for peace."

187

High demands,
I can't live up to.
You must be
my perfection or
you are nothing.
Adult strikes adult.
Painful distance.
"If you only knew today,
what is needed for peace."

National anxieties.
Playing the game,
trying to be in control,
asserting dominating power.
Irresponsible for destruction,
everyone pays and loses.
Death prevails.
"If you only knew today,
what is needed for peace."

Changes.
Either exchange one
dominance for another, or
have a change of heart.
One continues the game,
isolation, dominance prevail.
The other is servanthood.
Mutuality is what is needed today,
Christ's peace.

CW-H

Personal Reflection

A Story

Her name was frequently in the society columns as hosting important parties, cutting ribbons for openings, chairing the charity ball. She was catered to by her acquaintances and employees, lauded for her largesse and feared for her sharp and caustic tongue. She was always well-groomed, attractively coiffured, straight in posture, proud and arrogant.

Then came the rumor, a rumor that she was less than she seemed, that her roots were not among the social elite but among the social climbers. No matter that it was not true, that it was the result of a bitter but clever attack by someone she had snubbed. It was believed and she was snubbed in return.

She was not invited to important parties and the Important People stayed away from hers. She was not asked to cut ribbons and someone else was chosen to plan the charity ball. Her loyal employees left her to work for other people with equally caustic tongues but upon whom Society smiled.

There remained to her only one friend, a person she had often derided as too eager to please, too common. When she said to this eager, common woman, "Why are you still here?" The woman replied that it was because she detected real character and true kindness behind the arrogance and pride. This lone friend challenged her to look within her soul for acceptance and peace, the peace that comes from centering one's life on God, not on the world's acceptance.

And she believed and practiced what the eager, common woman taught. When the rumor was exposed, and Society would have returned her to her position in its fickle bosom, she did return to prominence in the community. She frequently hosted meetings bringing diverse groups together, she cut ribbons, and hosted charity fund raisers that reached far beyond Society's circles. She was loved by her friends and employees, blessed for her generosity, and thanked for her kind and helpful remarks. She was always well-groomed, attractively coiffured, straight in posture and as friendly and comfortable as an old shoe.

And rumor could no longer touch her. Her peace did not come from acceptance by her peers but from the knowledge that God accepted her and worked in and through her.

BJB

Biblical Character

Based on Luke 18:1-8

The Nagging Widow

Historically we know that widows of Jesus' day, similar to today, were given neither credibility nor social value. For a widow to be so presumptuous as to ask for her rights was quite incredible. What rights she was pleading for were really not relevant to the point that Jesus was trying to make. More than likely, however, they had something to do with her legal rights. Courts did not rule very favorably toward women in such cases as those dealing with money, inheritance, or property.

The widow probably already knew that the odds were against her. Her situation seemed hopeless, and society saw her as weak and powerless. Yet she did not let the hopelessness and society's view of her as weak take away her sense of justice, or deter her in her search for a change and acknowledgment of her rights and needs. She persisted to the point of being accused of being a "nag" or "a bitchy woman"—another way to try to control her. She was not going to let this man who represented the powerful male establishment control her by taking away her rights.

This passage, of course, is about our being persistent in prayer, but it is also about being persistent with people especially those who have no respect for other people or God. Our persistence may not appear to be getting us any place. Like the woman, we may have to keep going back to the establishment in order to create a positive change. Those in power have no reason to give up their control benevolently, even for the betterment of society, because they may have no respect for people or for God. They may only be interested in themselves. The widow seemed to know this. The judge ruled in her favor, not out of goodness or what was right, but rather because she was irritating him. Jesus, Ghandi, and Martin Luther King, Jr. were persons who were well aware of the power of persistence. They shook society at its very roots in order to get "our rights." This persistence can be very threatening to those in power, and they may try to control the other through violence. This is the way of the world and its understanding of peace. A cheap, unauthentic peace.

The woman may have become tired, desperate, or felt alone in her cause. Yet she didn't give up until justice was served. This woman and her courage to face and challenge the negative odds can be a challenge and inspiration to those fighting for justice and peace today.

CW-H

Historical Character

Beth Glick-Rieman

Late one night Beth Glick-Rieman and her husband were in bed when the door bell rang. She thought they had decided to ignore it and was surprised about ten minutes later to hear her husband coming up the stairs with someone. She heard him say, "I'll get it for you, please don't wake my wife." They entered the room and flipped on the light. Beth saw a man with a knife at her husband's back. Her husband's face was a pale gray. His upper lip was beaded with sweat. Fear filled her. He was a heart patient.

The stress might be too much for him. Somewhere deep within her she remembered Sadie and Ireland.

191

She had been one of 105 United States representatives who went to Ireland on the Journey of Reconcilation. They had stood with the Peace People at Boyne River to try to reconcile north and south Ireland. They literally went into the midst of the war.

While in Ireland, Beth stayed with Sadie Johnson, a very courageous woman. Sadie told her many stories of her fear and how she learned to confront it in order to go on living. She used to live in the fear that some Protestant would come to her door with a weapon and want to kill her or her family. So they lived behind locked doors. Finally she and her husband decided this was no way to live life, and she started to invite Protestant women, "the enemy," into her home. Then, people started to appear at her door with weapons because she was threatening their system of violent "separateness." One day when her husband didn't return home as expected, she looked for him and found him held at gun point by three men who wanted to take their car to make a bomb. She was very afraid, yet she trusted her belief in life. She confronted the men, asking them to put their guns down. She conversed with them as if they were reasonable men. She and her husband were able to drive their car home. This story of faith greatly moved Beth and proved her interconnectedness with Sadie. She was strengthened and prepared for this moment.

"Take that knife out of his back, he's a heart patient and you are frightening him. I don't like his being frightened." She gently pushed the intruder's hand down.

The man cursed in anger when he learned that her husband had only eighteen dollars. She told him she had some money in her purse downstairs. She asked if her husband could stay upstairs; his heart might not take another climb. The robber made them both go. He pressed the knife against her back. She stopped and said, "If you want your money you are going to have to take the knife out of my back and be more gentle with me." He removed the knife. After he got the money she asked him to leave. He refused.

"I don't like what you're doing," she said. "Look at my husband!" Her husband lifted his face from his hands so the robber could see his pallor.

"Hey, you are a sick old man, you need to see a doctor." He was a Jeckle and Hyde.

"Would you please leave now?"

"No! You just want to call the police."

After she assured him she was only interested in taking care of her husband and calling a doctor, he moved toward the door. "I hope you never do this again." He shook their hands and left. A month later she read that he was convicted of 20 burglaries and the murder of another couple like them. She discovered that she could show trust beyond reason, to face her fear and to be at peace.

Beth understands peacemaking as an "interconnectedness and an inner trust in life and others." She believes the world views peace as something that is attained and kept through force and fear.

Beth strongly believes that Christ did not come into the world to bring peace as the world knows it but to bring a sword of justice, truth, and equality. "The sword cuts through the systems of relating we have developed. We are then able to recognize the pain that is there and are free to change. This involves risk."

Several other incidents in her life also led Beth to greater faith and trust and to being a peacemaker for God. When she was about eight years old her grandfather died. She saw the anguish of his daughters including her mother. This was the first time she really saw people in pain. Yet, when the funeral came she was amazed and shocked to hear the enthusiasm with which the song "Oh, Happy Day," was sung. She wondered how these people who were in such pain could be singing this song with such intensity. She realized they had a deep comfort: their trust and sense of peace in knowing that life and God are good.

When Beth was fifteen, she and her youth group climbed to the top of a mountain. As she sat there watching the sunset, she was filed with a sense of rightness over the world. She took on a deep commitment that she could trust the creative process on earth which pulls and magnetizes each to life. This concept is central to the human family.

Another experience which helped shape her beliefs in justice and peacemaking occurred when she was twenty-seven. Her brother was killed in a car accident. When she saw her father, he, weeping, embraced her and said, "I do not doubt the Love of God." A great sense of inner peace came over her. She no longer resented the person who killed her brother, but rather found that she could rest in the power of the universe.

Many women and men have attributed to Beth the beginning of positive change in their lives. Beth has tried to help others to realize their interconnectedness and inner power to create greater peace in the world and in people's lives. This has caused her to be considered a threat by systems that are oppressive. At the women's gatherings of 1977 at Elizabethtown Church of the Brethren and 1978 at Manchester College, Beth facilitated women in releasing their power. Many believe that this work for change caused her to pay the "price of a peacemaker," to be made a scapegoat and asked to leave her job.

Beth Glick-Rieman now lives in California, still leading conferences and writing, still promoting the kind of peace in which she believes.

CW-H

Worship Resource

Litany

One: Peace I leave with you;
Another: I do not leave escape from trouble and a quiet life.
One: My peace I give unto you;
Another: If you will give your whole self to God, as I have done, no matter what comes to you, you will overcome with a quiet spirit.
One: Not as the world giveth, give I unto you.
Another: My peace no one can seize from you for it is internal and eternal.
One: Let not your heart be troubled,
Another: Even if you fail utterly, if you trust in God my peace is there.
One: Neither let it be afraid.
Another: In the midst of life's storms you may walk in my strength, my light, my peace.
One: Peace I leave with you.

BJB

Prayer

O God,

Send thy freeing, inner peace to rescue us from the tensions that tempt us to snap back at loved ones.

Send thy overflowing, enlightening peace to save us from the distance that separates us from those who should be friends.

Send thy strengthening, warming peace to deliver us from the anxieties our nation seems to court in its preoccupation with secret wars and rumors of wars.

Send thy cohesive, surrounding peace to free us from our need to dominate and control others.

Help us to look within thy word, thy love, and our own soul's response to that love. Help us to know the things that make for peace. Amen

BJB

Overcoming Walls

Ephesians 2:12-16

. . . remember that you were at that time separated from Christ, alienated from the commonwealth of Israel, and strangers to the covenant of promise, having no hope and without God in the world. But now in Christ Jesus you who once were far off have been brought near in the blood of Christ. For Jesus is our peace, who has made us both one, and has broken down the dividing wall of hostility, by abolishing in Christ's own flesh the law of commandments and ordinances to create in Christ's own flesh one new being in place of two, so making peace, so that we might both be reconciled to God in one body through the cross, thereby bringing the hostility to an end.

RSV adapted

Biblical Interpretation

In My Four Walls

The New Testament makes clear that everyone is my neighbor, not just the person living next door, but also those of a different nation, race or social status. I know this theoretically, but to put love into practice is difficult. I find myself "walled in"

. . . behind the walls of economic injustice.
My sister in India has no money to feed her growing family. My brother in Guatemala works hard to make a living, but the land he used to farm has been taken away. I own a car, a carpeted home, a

refrigerator full of food. My brothers and sisters have no roof overhead and are watching their children starve. Am I loving my neighbors when I enjoy my wealth while they have nothing?

. . . behind the wall of prejudice.
People tend to be suspicious of the unfamiliar. Why not learn from one another? Differences could be a source of exciting discovery, enriching and allowing us to grow. Instead, we hold on to preconceived notions and see differences as a threat. Am I loving my neighbors when I reject them because they are not like me?

. . . behind the wall of egocentricity.
Selfishness, some say, is linked to the survival instinct. But the Christian message is that all human beings are of equal worth to God. My life is not more precious than that of my sisters and brothers. Jesus identified with the least of these. Am I loving my neighbors when I think of my own interest first?

. . . behind the wall of idolatry.
We live in a time where idol worship abounds. We glorify the nation, state, wealth, and military power; and we don't hesitate to sacrifice human life in order to uphold these idols. Is it loving my neighbors when I contribute to weapon systems which will destroy them?

These walls keep me from living the life God wants me to live. I am paying too high a price: hurting others because I negate their humanity, and hurting myself because I cut myself off from my brothers and sisters.

Jesus, the Bible tells us, has broken down the enmity which stood like a dividing wall between us. If only we could learn to believe it and act accordingly!

Blessings!   IR

Ingrid Rogers

Literary Interpretation

The Stone Wall

(Dedicated to my friend Heidrun on the other side of the Iron Curtain and to people like her on either side.)

Characters

Group 1: Betty and Bob and their daughter, Barbara, Bob's sister Brenda, and their friend Bill, and his brother Ben

Group 2: Dick and Dora and their son Don, Dora's sister Darlene and their friends David and Dwight

Staging

No costuming or stage sets or furniture are needed. Imagine the stones and the wall. An open area for the stage and at least two aisles through the audience are all that are necessary except for a sign that says "TEN YEARS LATER" to be held up at the beginning of Scene 2.

Scene 1

Bob and Dick start collecting imaginary stones on opposite sides of the stage area. They pile the stones higher and higher. The dialogue runs parallel, switching from one group to the other.

Bill enters and walks up to Bob

Bill: Hey, what are you doing, Bob?

Bob: Time to start protecting myself. I don't trust those people over there.

David comes and approaches Dick.

David: Hey, Dick, what are all the stones for?

Dick: See that fellow over there? He's been piling them up for a while. Makes me nervous. I know he's getting ready to throw them at me. So I'm getting ready to defend myself, if need be.

Bob: Don't just stand there, Bill. Get busy. When they start throwing stones, you'll get it, too, you know.

Bill: Yeah, I guess you're right.

Bill bends over and starts helping

Bill: Maybe I should get my brother Ben to help me, too.

Bill goes off and returns with Ben.

Dick: Go get Dwight, will you? Looks like they are increasing their workers over there. We'd better be prepared when it all breaks loose.

198

David: I hate those folks over there. Why can't they leave us alone?

David leaves to get Dwight. Betty appears next to Bob.

Betty: Now what's gotten into you? Are you crazy? Wasting all day with those dumb stones. Who's going to get the farmwork done?

Bob: Oh, Betty, you need to get your priorities straight. What good will the farmwork do us when they have killed us all? Look at that pile of stones over there. Can't you tell what's up?

The men continue piling up stones. Dora comes up to Dick.

Dick: It's about time you got here, Dora. We are going to run out of stones soon. They have better resources over there. I need our household money to buy some more stones.

Dora: You've got to be kidding! How can I give you the household money for stones? What are we supposed to use for food, pray tell?

Dick: Better to tighten our belts a little than be destroyed by those people over there. If they can do it, we can, too.

The men continue to pile up stones.

Scene 2

Ten years later. (Someone walks across the stage with the sign "Ten Years Later.")

Barbara and her aunt Brenda come onto the "B" area of the stage, and Don and his aunt Darlene come onto the other.

Barbara: Hey, Aunt Brenda, what's behind that big wall?

Brenda: Bad people, little one. Very bad, ungodly people.

Barbara: Why, Aunt Brenda?

Brenda: They want to kill us baby. Some people are just mean, you know. You don't understand that yet.

Don: Why do Dad and Dwight keep working on that wall, Aunt Darlene?

Darlene: To protect you, Don.

Don: Protect me from what?

Darlene: From the bad people that live on the other side of the wall.

Don: But the wall is so high already! Aren't we protected enough?

Darlene: So long as they keep working on the wall, we have to, also.

Don: What do you think the people are really like over there?
Darlene: Hush, Don. They are bad people. Don't ask any more
            questions.

Scene 3

As Bill, Bob, and Ben go up one aisle, they talk to the people and
shout out the slogans below. Dick, David, and Dwight do the same
in the other aisle. Each repeats the slogans over and over while
moving around. Both groups use the same sentences but don't say
them at the same time.

Bill/Dick: Give to the great cause. Help protect our families
            from the enemy.
Bob/David: Don't worry about unemployment or education. Help
            us pile up the stones. Do this for democracy and free-
            dom! Only $200 billion a year!

Scene 4

Betty and Dora are asleep on the floor, each on her own side of the
wall.

Betty sits up.

Betty: Only 5 a.m. I wish I could sleep some more. There is so
            much on my mind. All anyone seems to care about is that
            cursed wall! Sometimes I want to go and see what they
            are really like over there.

Betty lies down again. Dora sits up and yawns.

Dora: Morning already! I wish I didn't have to face it. All this
            worry and always feeling so afraid. Sometimes I wonder
            why we couldn't just tear that wall down. Would they
            really throw stones at us if we did that?

Betty sits up again.

Betty: I wonder if there are women over there who are just as
            upset about this stone wall as I am.
Dora: If only I could let someone over there know how I feel.

Both stand up and begin to move toward the wall. Each climbs up
on the wall. Suddenly they notice each other. As they do, they look
terrified. Then they slowly nod their heads for a greeting.

Betty: (slowly, hesitatingly) Hi!
Dora: Hi!
Betty: (still looking scared) Are you . . . are you from over
            there?
Dora: Yes . . . and you?

Betty nods her head.

Dora: Do you . . . have children?

Betty: Yeah, we have two—Barbara and Belinda.

Dora: We have three—two boys and a girl. Don, the oldest, just started school.

Betty: Funny that we can talk to each other, isn't it?

Dora: They say over here that you're going to kill us.

Betty: Oh, that's what they tell us about you, too.

Dora: But . . . you look friendly!

Betty: I guess we just haven't had a chance to look at each other, face to face . . .

They reach out and join their hands.

Betty: What if we went back . . .

Dora: and told them . . .

Betty: that it all isn't true . . .

Dora: and that we both have children . . .

Betty: children who need food . . .

Dora: and jobs . . .

Betty: and life.

Dora: Yes! Life! A future in peace without fear!

They embrace and say together as they walk away from each other:

Betty/Dora: Let us tell them quickly!

IR

Personal Reflection

The Wall

Words and Music by Ingrid Rogers

1. A man had a neigh-bor whom he could not stand. He
2. As soon as the neigh-bor saw the man's in - tent, he
3. The wives had he - si - ta - tions to lend a help - ing hand, but
4. After sev'ral ge - ne - ra - tions it was al - most too late to
5. One day two lit - tle child - ren, one from eith - er side, started

en - vied him his gar - den and he en - vied him his land; and he
too start - ed build - ing, and he called a friend. Both sides
men said, "Come get bus - y! You just don't un - der - stand. Just
start mak - ing peace and to give up on their hate. The
climb-ing the wall to see what it would hide. When they

grew in his ha - tred af - ter man - y ver - bal fights o - ver
dou - bled their for - ces to ap - pear big and strong, no one
look at the ag gression of those peo-ple and their kin! If
wall had drained re-sources and seemed ve - ry ob - so - lete, and their
no - ticed each oth - er, they both want - ed to play, and they

child-ren and poss - ess - ions and pro - per - ty rights. So
want-ed to stop or ad - mit be - ing wrong. Soon
we do not de - fend ourselves, their side is apt to win. So the
child-ren had no jobs, and lit - tle to eat. But
did - n't care too much what their par - ents would say. They had

one day he de - cid - ed it was time to build a wall: Brick up - on brick,
all their pre - cious mon-ey was spent to build the wall: Brick up - on brick,
wo - men com-plied and the pro-ject could pro-ceed: Brick up - on brick,
still the race con-tin-ued. The wall went up some more: Brick up - on brick,
heard them talk of "en - e-mies" but learned that in the end Brick up - on brick,

lay-er, af - ter lay-er, 'cause he felt not pro-tect-ed at all.
lay-er, af - ter lay-er, un - til it stood strong and tall.
lay-er, af - ter lay-er, till the wall was tall in - deed.
lay-er, af - ter lay-er, in the in - ter - est of cold war.
lay-er, af - ter lay-er, the wall had hid-den a friend.

Biblical Character

Matthew 15:21-28

The Canaanite Woman

How my heart reaches out to the woman of Canaan! I want to protect her or console her, as she bears the onslaught of prejudice, abuse, and ridicule. Yet I know that woman does not need my protection. She can fend for herself, and she does it admirably well.

No socially erected barrier can hold her back when it comes to pleading for the life of her child. Her concern for her sick daughter makes her cry out in agony, and love propels her forward. Never mind that one should not shout after somebody. Never mind her society insisting that men should not talk to her in public. Never mind that she is not from the house of Israel and therefore has no business asking Jesus for help. For the sake of her child, she forgets about tradition and social taboos. She runs after Jesus, begs for help, even talks back as Jesus hesitates. Courageously she bears the degrading treatment of the disciples who scorn her behavior and want to be rid of her. With amazing mental agility she turns a cutting insult into a faith statement: "The dogs eat the scraps that fall from their master's table." With wit and persistence she fights for the life of another human being—and wins.

I admire her motherly devotion, her willingness to suffer maltreatment for the sake of justice, her ability to put more value on human life than on social customs or the law. She is committed, intelligent, selfless, strong—truly a model for us all.

IR

Historical Character

Yvonne Dilling

No walls separate us more than economic ones. In 1981, Yvonne Dilling sought to overcome these barriers by traveling to Central America in order to learn from the poor. She understood her journey as a pilgrimage. Aware of the struggles and injustices in those countries, her goal was to experience this life herself. In Honduras, the Catholic Charity organization Caritas invited her to stay as a volunteer and help them organize an education program for Salvadoran refugee children. Soon after her arrival a military groundsweep on the Salvadoran side of the border caused a new wave of refugees to pour into Honduras. Overnight, 3000 new people had to be provided with food, shelter, and medical aid in a rural mountain village miles away from any paved road. Yvonne was part of a team of swimmers which, under gunfire from Salvadoran helicopters, pulled children across the border river into safety. As a medical technician, she cared for the wounded and sick. Before resuming her educational tasks, she helped the Caritas team set up a tent city near the border.

In July of 1981, the Salvadoran army, with tacit approval from the Honduran government, invaded the Honduran border area and turned it into a militarized zone. They wanted no further refugees to flee across the river. Yvonne witnessed the mounting hostility on the part of the military, which finally culminated in the brutal murder of two of her co-workers. In December 1981, all refugees had to be relocated further inland for safety reasons. Yvonne accompanied them to a new camp, where she again set up an education program for the children.

Yvonne's experiences in Honduras are told in the book, *In Search of Refuge*, which she co-authored after her return to the United States. Her prophetic witness on behalf of the poor in Central America continues. She presently serves as Nicaragua coordinator for "Witness for Peace," a group which maintains a continuous non-violent, prayerful presence of United States citizens on the Nicaragua-Honduras border in order to prevent CIA-backed efforts to destabilize and overthrow the government.

What can we learn from Yvonne's story? She herself feels she has done little; for her the real heroes are the people of Central America who maintain a spirit of love in the midst of war, and who endure persecution without losing courage and hope. But Yvonne is a model for me. She did not talk about her faith but lived it. With women like her, walls no longer seem insurmountable.

IR

Worship Resource

A Litany in Celebration of our Sisters

One: Throughout history, women have stood up against that which creates or perpetuates injustice. They knew that all people have been invited to partake in the promise, and that as Christians we should not abuse, neglect, or violate any human being. Today we celebrate the women who have tried to break down the walls of prejudice and fear:
Rosa Parks who witnessed against racial segregation when she refused to give up her seat on a crowded bus in Montgomery, Alabama . . .

All: We are thankful for the leadership of Rosa Parks.

One: Yvonne Dilling, the coordinator of "Witness for Peace," who works for justice in Central America . . .

All: We are thankful for the leadership of Yvonne Dilling.

One: Jeri Seese, imprisoned because she prayed in public to witness against nuclear weapons . . .

All: We are thankful for the leadership of Jeri Seese.

This litany is not complete. You who are gathered for worship will recall other women whose courageous witness has had an impact on you. Give her name and state briefly how that woman has contributed to overcoming walls. After your statement, the group will respond, "We are thankful for the leadership of . . ." Be sure not to mention only nationally

205

known women, but also personal friends—those who have been guides in your own life. We can all contribute to breaking down the barriers which stand between us.

IR

Prayer

Benediction

Go now and be aware that Jesus overcame the walls which separated Jew and Gentile, owner and slave, men and women.
Go now and proclaim to the world that the walls have fallen:
—no more shall we allow wealth to keep us from identifying with the poor;
—no more shall anyone convince us that human beings we don't even know are our enemies;
—no more shall skin color or sex make one person feel inferior to another.
Be reconciled as one in Christ. Embrace as sisters and brothers.
Go now in peace.

IR

ACKNOWLEDGMENTS

The following people are gratefully acknowledged as contributors to THE WOMEN AT THE WELL.

Helen Howes Annan: Teacher, retired and living in Bridgewater Retirement Village; major interests: history, literature, volunteer work with mediation, peace movement, women's advocacy.

Cindy Brenize Booz: M.S. in Library Science, Library Media Specialist in Orange County, FL, elementary school. Wife, mother of two daughters.

Pamela Brubaker: M.Phil. (1986) Union Theological Seminary, New York, where she is completing a Ph.D. in Christian Social Ethics. Author of *She Hath Done What She Could: A History of Women's Participation in the Church of the Brethren*, she is active in advocating on behalf of women's full participation in church and society.

Betty Jo Buckingham: Ph.D. in Library Science, Consultant in the Iowa Department of Education, currently board president in her district and editor of *Women at the Well*.

Maria Elena Caracheo: Served as translator for Olga Serrano's contribution. Serves on the denomination's General Board staff.

Ann E. Cheeks: Graphic Designer for cover and layout of the book.

Barbara G. Cuffie: Feminist, liberated, happy mother who through the church and its people experienced a new dimension in her life so that being a black female became irrelevant. The discovery of having been created in God's image enabled her to love and care for herself and others, knowledge that is central to her life.

Esther Pence Garber: Retired teacher and author of *Button Shoes* and *Counting My Buttons*.

Judith L. Georges: M.Div., Pacific School of Religion (1984) and pastor of the Ivy Farms Church of the Brethren, Newport News, VA.

Peg Gibble-Keenan: Completing MA in social work and working with emotionally disturbed children. She spent her Brethren Volunteer Service assignment in N. Ireland where she met and married her husband. Mother of one son.

Beth Glick-Rieman: MA, D.Min., Free-lance writer, speaker, consultant and workshop leader in areas of social justice, empowerment of women and peace. Director, HEIRS, Human Empowerment in Religion and Society, a feminist consultant firm based in Spring Valley, CA. For some, Beth is known as mentor, a woman of courage and uncompromising radical feminist principles. She thinks of herself as a woman dedicated to calling out the gifts of others.

Patricia K. Helman; A.B., McPherson College, KS, LitD. McPherson College; Author of *Free to be a Woman, In League with the Stones, At Home in the World;* Columnist for *Messenger*, Member of Board of Governor's of National Council of Churches, 1978-84, Moderator of South Central Indiana, 1982.

Jean Lichty Hendricks: M.Div. Bethany Theological Seminary, ordained minister in Church of the Brethren, active as pastor of local congregation in Lawrence, KS, wife, mother of two, student of "women's spirtuality."

Leona Ikenberry: Retired Christian Education Director, LaVerne Church of the Brethren. Former member of Womaen's Caucus Steering Committee, currently working on peace and justice issues.

Ruthann Knechel Johansen: Ph.D. in English, Asst. Professor of American Literature, currently living in Princeton Junction, NJ and writing a fictional narrative on plain women's language, a critical study of Flannery O'Connor's fiction, and a series of articles on one family's journey back from head injury. Mother & wife.

Pat Judd: Graduate of Juniata College, former teacher, wife and mother.

Marilyn Kieffaber: M.Ed. from University of Missouri. A pastor's wife, mother, and teacher living in Sidney, Ohio.

Shirley C. Kirkwood: Womaen's Caucus worker, hospice and mediation volunteer. Lives in Shenandoah Valley, VA.

Linda Logan: Christian Education Director in Harrisonburg, VA, and resource leader for Brethren World Peace Academy.

Elaine Hartman McGann: feminist, free spirit, lover of all Her creation.

Gena Tenney Phenix: BA Barnard College, living in Bridgewater, VA. Is an active volunteer in church and community welfare projects.

Nancy Werking Poling: Communications specialist for a consulting firm in Lombard, IL.

Ruby Rhoades: Born Ruby Frantz on June 1, 1923 and died January 8, 1985. She was married in 1943 to Benton Rhoades. They have four children and ten grandchildren.

Ingrid Rogers, Ph.D. in American Literature, D.Min. student in peace studies at Bethany Theological Seminary; author of books, plays, songs; pastor, mother and wife.

Olga Serrano: Pastor at the Rio Prieto Fellowship, Church of the Brethren, near Lares, Puerto Rico.

Jeanne Jacoby Smith: Director of publicity at McPherson College (KS), in doctoral program at Kansas State Univ., wife, mother of two sons.

Paula J. Stanley: Member of LaVerne, (CA) Church of the Brethren, former primary and pre-school teacher, presently a student enrolled at School of Theology at Claremont.

Jo Young Switzer: Ph.D. from University of Kansas (1980), teaches speech communication at Manchester College, (IN).

Beverly Weaver, M.Div. Bethany Theological Seminary. Working toward pastoral career, wife and mother of one son.

Cindy Weber-Han: M.Div., Bethany Theological Seminary. Counselor for rape, incest, and domestic violence. Co-pastors with husband in Council Bluffs, IA, mother of two. Served on Womaen's Caucus Steering Committee, involved in promoting equality and peace issues.

Dorothy Blanchard Wiggins: Retired director of Christian Education; wife, mother, local church moderator. Lives in and is active in social concerns of State College, PA.

Dawn Ottoni Wilhelm: M.Div. Princeton Theological Seminary (1986), a licensed minister and active member of Ambler Church of the Brethren. She is currently working as a chaplain in a residency program in Clinical Pastoral Education at Lehigh Valley Hospital Center, Allentown, PA. and is interested in women's issues and family and marriage counseling.

Lena Buterbaugh Willoughby: Graduate of University of LaVerne (CA). She and her husband serve as chaplains at Brethren Hillcrest Homes in LaVerne. Teacher, mother and wife, Lena has been actively involved in justice issues related to women and children.

Appendix

Scriptures

Biblical Characters

Historical Characters